D1603104

The Banditti of the Plains

OR THE CATTLEMEN'S INVASION OF WYOMING IN 1892—"THE CROWNING INFAMY OF THE AGES." WRITTEN BY A. S. MERCER IN 1894. THIS EDITION CARRIES A NEW FOREWORD BY JAMES MITCHELL CLARKE AND ILLUSTRATIONS BY ARVILLA PARKER.

PRINTED FOR GEORGE FIELDS OF SAN FRANCISCO BY THE GRABHORN PRESS : : : : MCMXXXV

Copyright 1935 by George Fields

PRINTED IN THE UNITED STATES OF AMERICA BY THE GRABHORN PRESS

Contents

I was somewhat startled to read that my father was a red-handed murderer.*

He died when I was four years old, and I grew up believing that he was a kindly man, good to his family and not such a person as would terrorize innocent settlers and drive them from their homes.

I had, of course, heard the story. My father came into Cheyenne on the train from the east. "Billy" Irvine met him. He said:

"Come on, Clarke. Get your bedroll and rifle. We're going up into Johnson county."

So my father went along, and Champion and Ray were killed, and the cattlemen were besieged in the T. A. ranch.

I had seen the cribbage board the "invaders" made out of a thick tug from a set of freight harness. My mother had told me the message my father sent by one of the men who got through the lines of the besiegers— "Remember that I love you."

The troops came to the T. A., but my father did not know that they would come. . . .

I knew that during the long-drawn trial of the cattlemen, my father's herds were plundered; that he abandoned the ranch which had taken twelve years in the building and went farther east until he could get capital for a fresh start in Montana.

* A. B. (Arthur Browning) Clarke, who came to Wyoming in 1877. His brand was "D. E." and his ranch was in Laramie county, at the base of the Black Hills.

All this happened long before I was born.

I thought, when I first read "The Banditti of the Plains" that it must be my mother's fault that I did not know that the Johnson County War was "the crime of the ages." My mother was a fragile woman who, curiously, loved Wyoming. My father, I thought, must have kept things from her. And I realized that an intense affection must have made her prejudiced.

I was surprised—I say—to read that the cattlemen intended to "kill off several hundred settlers and drive the rest from their homes." But A. S. Mercer's documentation and his logic seemed irrefutable.

In the library of Stuart N. Lake, the western historian, I found other accounts of the Johnson County War. Some of these are contemporary, some the work of historians. All substantially agree with the facts as narrated in "The Banditti of the Plains." But I was cheered to find that no one else placed the same interpretation upon the facts, or assigned the same purposes and motives to the "invaders." And as to the character of the citizens of Johnson county and conditions in Wyoming at the time, there is very sharp divergence at almost all points.

The early eighteen-eighties were years of spectacular profit in the range cattle industry. Investments paid as high as 30% in a single season and feverish speculation threw cattle by hundreds of thousands onto the Wyoming prairies. Following a hard winter in the Southwest, huge herds of Texas cattle were brought up in the summer of '86. Then, to an over-stocked range, came the winter of 1886-87, which still makes the eyes of old-timers turn bleak when they remember. In the spring, cattle were piled like driftwood along the gullies and the bitter bark of the willows was eaten as high as an animal could reach. One man who turned loose 2,500 head in the fall, gathered only 200, and losses of 80% were common.

That year the bottom fell out of the cattle market and many large companies operating in Wyoming went to the wall. In St. Louis the crash pulled down the biggest bank, and the shock was felt as far away as Europe—where cattle-speculating had been a rage. Cattle prices continued damagingly low, and many

Easterners and Europeans sold out and left. It was at this time
that Theodore Roosevelt gave up ranching.

Those who stayed to tough it out were most of them men like
my father; men who had grown up with the country. They were
harrassed by debts and their herds were only skeletons of what
they had been. They sold their cattle too young, but they did it
to save themselves from ruin, not to satisfy the avarice of eastern and foreign investors. Depleted herds were one cause of a
contraction in the range cattle industry. Another cause was a
growing conviction that the time was over when cattle could
be wintered profitably on the open range, without herding or
feeding.

By 1892, the year of the Johnson County War, the ranchers
needed less land than before and the transition from the old
careless methods of the open range to the modern way of planned
and controlled cattle-raising was well under way. But change
creeps on like old age and is never fully realized until accomplished. Neither the large-scale ranchers nor their enemies
realized fully what was taking place.

Wyoming cattlemen had from the earliest days, two chief
antagonists: weather and stock thieves. A hard winter in that
chill, blizzard-whipped country is like a drought in the wheat
belt—devastating. The rugged, broken terrain inevitably made
cattle hard to guard and offered perfect hiding places for
thieves. And the tremendous wealth-on-the-hoof which grazed
the public domain unwatched, drew the most able rustlers of
the country.

The Wyoming Stock Growers Association was formed, like
the associations of other cattle states, to regulate the industry
and to protect the property of its members. Like the others, it
rose from the need for cooperation and the necessity for doing
what the federal government was too lax and too distant to accomplish, and local government was too weak and corrupt to
take upon itself. The Wyoming Association was notable as the
largest, the most effective and the most powerful of them all.
In the long run it was too powerful for its own good.

The first of its acts to arouse antagonism was the "Maverick

bill" which the Association put through the Wyoming territorial legislature in 1884. This law set dates for the common
roundups and laid down rules for their conduct. It defined a
"maverick" as any unbranded calf running without its mother,
and provided for the sale of these estrays at public auction during the roundup's progress.

The law accomplished two things: it prevented "sooners"
from working over the cattle and running them thin before the
majority of owners got on the ground, and it discouraged the
"maverickers." So long as the ranges were uncrowded, "maver-
icking" was common practice and worked no hardship. An owner
was likely to get back the same number of estrays that he lost.
But when the herds of many outfits mingled on overlapping
ranges, regulation became imperative. Furthermore, there was
great temptation to make mavericks by driving the calves to
such a distant part of the range that they became permanently
separated from the cows which bore the identifying brand, or
by splitting the calf's tongue so that it could not suckle. The
"maverick law" effectually put a stop to these practices.

The antagonism to it was strong among men who had hoped
to build up their herds by appropriating estrays. Some members
of the Association had done this; why shouldn't they? And the
management of the roundups was placed by the law in the hands
of the Association. This seemed to many monopolistic and
unfair.

But resentment was hottest among those blacklisted by the
Association. The rules were stringent, and vigorously enforced.
No man whose record had stock-stealing in it could work for
any member of the Association. No man who was strongly suspected of being a rustler could buy mavericks at the public
auctions during the roundups. And, of course, no suspected
rustler could belong to the Association and receive its benefits.
Undoubtedly some judgments were unfair and certainly a few
men must have been blacklisted through the malice of Association members. But it has never been the practice of industry
to employ men with prison records or dubious associates

Another rule which caused bad feeling, and with more reason, was that which forbade a member of the Association to employ any man who owned cattle of his own. That this rule was fathered by Horace Plunkett — who later became one of the leading spirits of the "Irish Renaissance," which fostered both the Abbey Theatre and farmers' associations—indicates what lay behind it. The Europeans, most of them Britishers, came to Wyoming with the notion of feudal domains still in their minds. They operated on a large scale, and "absentee owner-ship" was common practice among them. During their almost continual absence they entrusted their affairs to foremen who actually ran their ranches. A foreman who owned no cattle could be trusted not to appropriate any from his employer's herds; *ergo* the rule against cattle-owning employees.

These foreigners had a knack for enraging the people among whom they lived. Their ranch houses were often luxurious in contrast to the log houses of their neighbors. When they came to Wyoming at all they came to hunt big game and enjoy them-selves rather than to ranch. And they did ostentatious things like keeping relays of fast horses for quick dashes across the country.

These were the "cattle barons." The term seems to be a catch phrase coined by Democratic politicos who were campaigning on the promise of "homes for poor men." Perhaps these poli-ticians were honest. Perhaps they thought that Wyoming was another Kansas or Nebraska and adapted to small-scale agricul-ture. Perhaps they did not understand that even the river bot-toms of Wyoming can be farmed only by expensive irrigation, and that most of the state is fit for nothing but large-scale graz-ing. At any rate, the "cattle barons" made a good target.

Most of the foreigners left after the disaster of 1886-87, and the remaining members of the Association had their backs to the wall. But the hue and cry against the "cattle kings" went on long after. And into Wyoming came hundreds of "settlers" or "grangers" to take up small tracts of the public domain which had been free range. It was natural that the cattlemen should be hostile to these Russian immigrants and trash from the older sections of the United States. But time after time the foremen and owners of the big outfits fed them when they arrived destitute. The settlers thanked them by shooting their cattle* and becoming their most bitter enemies. The politicians had made the image of the cattleman an ogre, and it was easy to turn the settler's bitterness at his own destitution and disappointment in an unfriendly country against those who were successful.

The forces arrayed against the Wyoming Stock Growers Association, then, were these: the men who had honest grievances; the local politicians; the settlers or grangers; the rustlers who used all the other anti-stock elements to clothe their thieving with the appearance of righteousness.

The resentment grew in the north where the grangers were most plentiful, where the herds of Association men were least protected and where the rustlers were boldest. And in 1888 this resentment began slowly to turn against the government. In that year, the territorial legislature created a board of livestock commissioners which set the time of roundups and regulated the industry in general. Since this commission was fostered by the Stock Growers Association, and took over many of the Association's old functions, Association and government became merged in the indignant mind of the public and gave further excuse for defying law.

The hand of the Board of Livestock Commissioners was not so strong as the old Association, and thieves flourished between 1888 and 1892. Many an honest cowboy who had found work scarce since '87 and many a hard-hit rancher turned to rustling in these years. The *Cheyenne Daily Leader*, which was not friendly to the stockmen, said in its issue of July 25, 1891:

"Men who before this year have borne and deserved good characters are now openly engaged in preying upon the public ranges. . . . All their neighbors and acquaintances are perfectly aware of the fact and the practice is oftentimes not merely winked at, but applauded. . . . Efforts have been made by some of the larger cattle companies to bring the offenders to justice.

*Letter of Harry Oelrichs, president of the Anglo-American Cattle Company to Sturgis, March 3, 1887; "The loss on Hat Creek through the farmers has been something frightful. They have not confined themselves to killing for their own use, but have killed wantonly. On one stretch of a mile and a half on Hat Creek, there are over thirty cattle dead, every one of which shows rifle or pistol wounds."

In some cases the grand juries have refused to indict; in others petit juries have brought in verdicts of not guilty in the face of evidence as conclusive and convincing as any ever submitted in a court of justice. . . . Small ranchmen have been terrorized into submission. They take good care to avoid seeing what is going on under their very noses and the reasons for doing so must be very obvious to everyone who knows anything of frontier life. . . . There are only two horns to the dilemma, either the thieves or the cattlemen must go."

The Wyoming Stock Growers Association again took the police power into its own hands. Stock detectives worked their way into rustler territory and collected evidence. When this evidence failed to obtain convictions in corrupt courts, there was little else that a frontier organization could do but use stronger methods. There is sufficient evidence in the Association records to warrant the belief that a few rustlers were "executed."

But there is no evidence that Ranger Jones and John Tisdale were bushwhacked by Association killers. The crime was charged to Frank Canton, but he was acquitted in Buffalo, county seat of Johnson county and the rustler capital. And there is nothing in Frank Canton's record as a peace officer either before or after to indicate that he was addicted to shooting from ambush. He did not need to hide to win his fights.

Who really killed these men was never learned, but the episode was like gasoline thrown on the fire of popular resentment. A rumor sprang up and spread over the northern counties to the effect that the Association cattlemen were planning to murder, burn and plunder until they had driven every granger and small ranchman from his home. And the Association detectives must have made mistakes which helped the rumor-spreaders. In a country where there were "rustlers who ranched on the side" and "ranchers who rustled on the side," Diogenes would have needed two lanterns.

All through 1891, stealing became more flagrant and the Association, in the fall of that year, got the Stock Commission to issue to its inspectors at market points an order to stop all shipments of cattle bearing the brand of a known rustler. The Association furnished a list of brands. Bills of sale were disregarded because the rustlers were known to use the grangers as fences. The cattle were held until ownership could be proved. If the shipper could not prove ownership they were sold, proceeds going either to the Livestock Commissioners or to the owners of the cattle from whom they had been stolen.

The procedure was undoubtedly high-handed and many honest ranchers and sincere journalists resented it. The rustler element howled and feeling in Johnson county rose to the exploding-point. In the early spring of 1892 a band of fifty armed men took over the town of Buffalo, and a rival organization known as the Northern Wyoming Farmers and Stock Growers Association was formed. This group sent a petition to Cheyenne demanding that the cattle held by the inspectors be released and the moneys returned to the shippers. This was refused on the grounds that honest and unwilling citizens had been coerced into signing the petition.

The next move in Johnson county was to post notices for a roundup on May first, one month earlier than the legal roundup date.

The "invasion" was organized to stop this "shotgun roundup." The Association men who planned it intended also to "execute" a number of rustlers against whom the Association detectives had found evidence. Warrants had been issued for the arrest of at least some of these men, and Frank Canton was appointed deputy United States marshal to serve them.

In spite of these precautions, the expedition was no more legal than the San Francisco Vigilantes of 1856. It was an attempt to protect property which the agencies provided by law did not safeguard. But it was too late for that kind of thing; in 1892 the United States was almost civilized.

When the cattlemen got into Johnson county, northern Wyoming rose up against them almost in a body. The rustlers came out to protect their trade, and they brought the grangers along to fight their old enemy. The rumors of 1891 were revived and some small ranchers and townsmen were convinced that the cattlemen had come to drive honest folk from their homes. A few must have joined the fight just for the hell of it.

The narrative of the fight at the K. C. ranch and the siege of the T. A., as told in "The Banditti of the Plains," agrees pretty well with other accounts. But in spite of the fact that their remains were eulogized and mourned in Buffalo, there is not much doubt that Nate Champion and Nick Ray were rustlers. Champion, perhaps, would be better served by an epitaph than a defense; he was as brave as any man on the northern plains, and bore the reputation of being the deadliest gunfighter in Wyoming. Other notable persons of the Johnson county faction were Arapahoe Brown—a little man who rose from obscurity to be their tactical expert—and Rev. M. A. Rader. Brown saved many lives by preventing the hot-headed besiegers from rushing the barricaded ranch. Rev. Rader was a Methodist divine of Buffalo who became popular after he thrashed a cattleman in a street brawl. His fiery oratory spurred the four hundred besiegers on. How the fight would have ended if the troops had not come is a matter of pure conjecture. The "go-devil" certainly could not have been brought close enough to be effective, and it is equally certain that a good hundred lives would have been lost; for the cattlemen would not have surrendered.

During the trial of the cattlemen, herds and ranch houses in northern Wyoming were plundered without mercy. When a committee in Buffalo invited the cattlemen to come up and look after their interests in the north, they sent a young deputy United States marshal named George Wellman. He was promptly shot. But the attempt to blame this killing on the Association (as set forth in "The Banditti of the Plains") was not so successful as in the deaths of Jones and Tisdale. Negro troops came to northern Wyoming and rustling waned.

But the political repercussions of the Johnson County War did not die till some time afterward. The Association supported the Republican office-holders; the anti-stock elements, the Democratic and Populist aspirants. In 1894 Asa Shinn Mercer —famous in his day because he imported three hundred brides-

to-be wholesale into Washington Territory and was for a brief
time president of Washington Territorial University when it
taught primary school children and college students with equal
zeal—wrote "The Banditti of the Plains." One has only to read
it to see that Mercer's intention was to damage as much as
possible the prominent Republicans of Wyoming. Even the
"confession" of Dunning, the Idaho man who hid in the attic
of the T. A. ranch house when the troops came and later wan-
dered into Buffalo, reads as much like a political pamphlet as
a narrative of events. The book had scarcely appeared when a
court order was handed down commanding that all the plates
and all copies remaining in the publishers' hands be destroyed.

Its subsequent rarity has made the book something of a myth.
Collectors have hoarded copies and a whisper has gone around
among historiophiles about "the book that gives the lowdown
on the cattle barons." It is a book of great interest and importance, but its effect has been somewhat sinister. Only in
recent years have books appeared which deal thoroughly and
impartially with the events, and these have not had the noto-
riety of "The Banditti of the Plains."

To bring A. S. Mercer's volume to light again is really an
act of justice to brave if injudicious men who cannot defend
themselves from the grave. For the modern reader is not likely
to see the "invasion" as the "crime of the ages." Now that hot
blood has cooled and those politicians and cattlemen are alike
dust, it is easier to see it as the dying blaze that ended the day
of the range cattle business and began its twilight.

The following pages have been written and tied together for the purpose of giving to the world the true story of the invasion of Wyoming's soil by the cattlemen of the plains. It is not sent out as a literary production, but an honest statement of the facts as they occurred. Personal acquaintance with the principal actors and accurate general knowledge of the country and its conditions, have given me unusual facilities for gathering reliable data. Every statement herein made is backed up by readily accessible proofs.

A. S. MERCER.

February 20th, 1894.

HE vast regions of country lying between the Missouri river on the east and the Sierra Nevada Mountains on the west, an area covering nearly two-fifths of the surface of the United States of America, was until recent years considered an unproductive waste, suited only to occupancy by wild beasts of prey, the bison and the Indian. In the "days of '49," when an almost unbroken line of wagons stretched across the plains, and for a decade following, it was supposed to be forever set apart as the summer grazing grounds of nature's untamed herds; to be the home of man—never.

About this time belated freight trains, drawn by hundreds of footsore oxen, were caught in the eastern foothills of the Rocky Mountains by the early snowfall. Human nature revolted at the suggestion, but there was nothing left for the train masters but to go into such winter quarters as they could construct, turning the dumb brutes loose on the creek bottoms to perish or live on such herbage as they could find. Many a tender-hearted frontiersman was moved almost to tears at the thought of his faithful beasts being left in the wilds as food for wolves. What, then, was their joy when the springtime came and the cattle were found not only to have escaped the fangs of the wolves and mountain lions, but to be fat and sleek, ready for the onward march.

These revelations becoming generally known, and mineral discoveries being made in the mountain valleys that attracted a considerable population of gold seekers, adventurous cattlemen brought herds from the old states and from the grassy plains of Texas to supply the mountain markets and the military posts scattered through the Indian country for the protection of the miners and immigrants. These herds all readily adapted themselves to their surroundings, grew and waxed fat, thus demonstrating that the grasses of the plains, the valleys and the foothills were of the most nutritious character. Ascertaining that no preparation of winter food was necessary for the roving herds, the whole region was soon filled with cattle, the farmers of the states and the ranchmen of Texas were all called upon to contribute to the great herds being located wherever grass and water could be found in juxtaposition. These herds numbered all the way from one thousand head up to fifty thousand, and in two or three instances over a hundred thousand were claimed by one company. The price of beef ruled high on the Eastern markets, and for a time all the ranchmen made money rapidly. The cost of caring for, or "running" a herd was lessened in proportion to the increase in numbers, and this necessarily led to consolidations by purchase or the formation of companies and the absorption of small herds. Large dividends were declared and a craze for cattle company investments was created in the East and also in the British Isles. Soon the bulk of the holdings passed into the hands of corporations and high-salaried officers took charge of the business, living luxuriously at the club houses in the various towns and trusting the real management of the herds and ranches to subordinates, sometimes with, but more frequently without, practical experience.

This was all very well while the markets ruled high and a thousand-pound steer brought, at the Chicago stock yards, sixty to seventy dollars. If expenses piled up and the output of ripe steers in the autumn was likely to prove inadequate for the meeting of current expenses and the declaring of the usual annual dividend on the stock, a bunch of two-year-old steers and the culls from the threes and fours, unfit for beef, were rounded up, shipped and sold as feeders, the proceeds going to swell the regular profits on the business and cheer the heart of the stockholder. This robbery of the herd was all right from the managers' standpoint so long as it tickled the avarice of the Eastern or foreign shareholders and prevented a careful investigation of the methods employed. But it was wholesale robbery just the same, and sooner or later must be discovered and charged up to those responsible therefor.

Meantime the country was virtually overrun with cattle, the ranges crowded and the grass eaten until the winter food was too short to carry the stock through the cold weather.

The range cattle industry is based on the theory and fact that the grasses of the so-called arid region grow up in the spring, quickly ripen and cure in the sun, retaining all of the sugar, starch, gluten, etc., in a more or less crystalized state, thus affording a really rich winter diet for all kinds of herbivorous animals. So long as the requisite proportion of the growth was allowed to mature and properly cure, the cattle thrived in winter nearly as well as in summer—at least they remained strong and healthy during the stormy weather and quickly laid on flesh when the green grass came. With the range overcrowded the grass was largely consumed in summer and very little was left to grow tall and carry rich seeds for winter feeding. The winter range should not be grazed in summer.

This shortage of feed, coupled with a few exceptionally hard winters, caused an excessive mortality among all classes of cattle and reduced the calf crop fully one-half in all the mixed, or breeding herds. Very soon this commenced to tell in the output of beef steers and greatly reduced the income of the company, so that more robbery of the herd had to be resorted to in order to pay a dividend and keep up the market price of the stock shares.

Then came a sudden and marked decline in beef values at the great market centers. The steers that had brought anywhere from fifty to seventy dollars at Chicago, now sold for from twenty-five to fifty, a shrinkage of nearly one half as a rule. This decline was due first, to the real falling off in beef values, and second to the generally poor condition of the range shipments in consequence of over-stocking and the resulting scarcity of feed.

Under these circumstances the company managers were forced to ship beef steers, dry cows and heifers, every fat, available

two-year-old and sometimes the thrifty yearlings, in order to
balance the expense and dividend account. But to these temporary makeshifts there must eventually come an end. Thus it is
evident that the general managers of cattle companies found
themselves in exceedingly hot water—between the devil and the
deep sea, so to speak. Something had to be done; their integrity
and financial reputation demanded action. Dividends were passed
and shareholders demanded the reason. To explain that the
herds had been systematically robbed of future beef steers in
the shipment of unripe cattle would be to impeach themselves.
To admit that the hard winters and overstocking of ranges had
decimated the herds would not be in harmony with official reports rendered. Some other excuse must be found. Eureka, says
one. "Thieves!" he ejaculated, and forthwith the cry echoed and
re-echoed over the entire range cattle country. Of the evolutions
following this remarkable discovery, a description will be given
in another chapter.

Cattle and horse stealing are old industries, older than modern civilization. Christ was crucified between thieves, and the
books of Moses are not silent on this ancient and modern accom-
plishment. Cattle stealing on the ranges by means of changing
the brands has been practiced to a certain extent by a limited
number of disreputable people ever since the beginning of the
range cattle industry, and it will always continue. The enact-
ment of laws restrains, but it does not prevent crime. As a matter
of fact there is less stealing and less lawlessness generally on
the plains of the West than in any other part of the world.
However contrary to the general theory that our advancing civilization is elevating and refining it may seem, it is nevertheless
true that with the increase of years and population there is an
increased percentage of crime. The great mass of Wyoming's
population is made up of honest men and women, as the following figures from the United States census report of 1890 fully
establish:

While the Northeastern states, which are supposed to be most civilized, and with the least number of criminals, have just 1,600 prisoners
to the million of people, Wyoming has only 1,200 to the million—one-

fourth less. The states and territories from Nebraska to the Pacific average 2,200 prisoners to the million; but Wyoming scarcely more than half this. Idaho has 1,700 to the million; Colorado, 2,200; California, 2,800—Wyoming has a remarkably small ratio—nearly three times as many. Nevada, with one-fourth less population than Wyoming, has 3,300, two and three-fourths times as many; Arizona, with about the same population as Wyoming, has 4,200, three and one-fourth times as many offenders as Wyoming.

Geographical comparison is equally striking. Wyoming is larger than Massachusetts, New York, New Hampshire, Vermont, Connecticut, Rhode Island, Maryland, New Jersey, Delaware and the District of Columbia. While these communities had in 1890, 23,000 prisoners, Wyoming had only 74. Wyoming is larger than Maine, Pennsylvania and Maryland put together, yet while these old, well-settled states had 7,000 criminals, all that great region had but one-hundredth part as many. Even little Delaware had nearly double the number of criminals that Wyoming had, and little Rhode Island, about one-ninetieth the size of Wyoming, had over seven times as many. Massachusetts had seventy times as many; New York, 1,400 times as many.

The few scalawags who live by plundering their neighbors are generally confined to the villages and towns where they can dispose of their ill-gotten gains. Considering the fact that the hundreds of thousands of cattle running on our plains and mountain sides are rarely seen by their owners, or herders, more than once a year, at the general round-up, when the calves are branded with the character or letter worn by their mother, the small loss from theft is not only remarkable, but a high testimonial to the good character of our people.

The livestock industry of Wyoming has been the leading pursuit for more than a double decade of years, and the stockmen have dominated the political and financial policy of the territory from its establishment in 1868 down to 1892. The Legislature has always been largely made up of livestock owners or local representatives of Eastern and foreign cattle syndicates, and until the last session of that body, in January, 1893, the laws have been framed to suit the manipulators of the stock interest. In 1872 the Wyoming Stock Growers' Association organized, the membership comprising most of the leading stock growers of the commonwealth and many citizens from the adjoining territories. This body was a strong, centralized power, and for years virtually shaped the territorial policy and socially controlled throughout the realm. Legislative enactments first assumed form in the councils of the Executive Committee of the Association and through its social prestige were popularized with the masses, even before adoption as laws. Thus, through the agency of the Stock Association and the stockmen in the several legislatures, the stock-growing industry was in full command of the law-making department. Naturally they everywhere dominated. The people acquiesced because of the magnitude of the cattle interest.

About 1889 conditions began to change. The people became restless under existing policies and demanded a new deal in the interest of the masses. Settlements had formed along the valleys in the northern and central portions of the state, where water could be had for irrigation purposes, and comfortable country homes were already in existence, with the promise of many ac-cessions in the near future and the making of prosperous and happy communities. The settlers by far outnumbered the cattle-men, and they, quite reasonably, thought they had some rights the cattlemen were bound to respect. More or less friction re-sulted, for which, in all human probability, some blame attaches to both parties. Notwithstanding this condition of affairs the country continued prosperous in a fair degree, and the new homes were being made along all the water courses. This was the situation up to the time of the invasion, the description of which appears in succeeding chapters.

For the better understanding of the general reader, it is per-haps advisable to explain more in detail the difference between the conditions surrounding the range cattle business in its early existence and those prevailing during the period immediately preceding and leading up to the time of the invasion. In the early days the country was open from Montana to Texas; the plains and foothills were well set in grass; the streams gener-ally were partially or fully lined with brush and the cattle roamed at will, finding abundant food everywhere. When a bliz-zard from the north prevailed the animals headed south and walked until the storm ceased, sometimes going more than a hundred miles without stopping. When the storm was over the tired cattle lay down to rest. A few hours later, disturbed by the pangs of hunger, they rose, turned their heads towards their home range and quietly grazed on their way north. Did not a second blizzard interpose and drive them further south, the warm days of spring would find most of the herd on its accustomed feeding grounds. Did the winter prove severe and storm follow storm in rapid succession, the cattle would be found hundreds of miles from their home range at the spring round-up, whence they would be sent back by the cowboys. Instances are of record where Wyoming cattle drifted during the winter three hundred miles, to the Arkansas river. The general round-up system in vogue all over the range country made the return of drifted cattle almost a certainty. Thus, the losses were merely nominal, and the herds were in good condition each spring.

During the latter period under review material changes had come about. The luxuriant growth of grass was found only in small areas; the brush along the streams was largely destroyed, so that browsing, that in the early days saved the lives of thousands of cattle, was no longer a resource; the homeseeker had squatted along the rich valleys, and long lines of wire fences obstructed the free movement of cattle before the storm; the railroad lands had been sold and largely fenced, thus more effectually hemming-in the storm-pushed animals. A striking pecularity of the range-raised cattle is that if you destroy the perfect liberty of action they at once become dependent—lose their will power and rustling qualities. Illustrative of this numerous instances could be cited where range cattle, drifting before a storm, came upon a fence that they could not pass through and in utter helplessness walked back and forth along the fence until they fell exhausted, one upon another, and died by the hundred.

With their ranges restricted and fence obstructions on all sides, it became evident to cattle owners that the open range business must soon be reduced to a matter of history, or the settlements in the country be discouraged and the obstructions removed. The paramount question was: "Which of these conditions shall be permitted to materialize?"

Stockmen complained bitterly of the failure of the courts to convict persons indicted or arrested for the theft of cattle and made this their rallying cry. There was a very potent reason for whatever truth these allegations contained.

Up to 1884 cowboys were chosen with an eye to their expertness in the use of the rope and branding iron. In addition to their regular monthly wages it was quite common for herd owners to pay the boys from $2.50 to $5 per head for all the "mavericks" they could put the company's brand on, and "rustling for mavericks" in the spring was in order all over the range country. It is currently reported that one cattleman, now high in political preferment, raised the price to $7.50 per head, and in consequence made what newspapermen call a "scoop" on his brethren, who tarried behind in the $5 list.

This practice taught the cowboy to look upon the unbranded, motherless calf as common, or public property, to be gathered in by the lucky finder.

Spurred on by the secret practice of a few cattlemen in advancing the price of mavericks to cowboy rustlers, the stock association prepared the "Maverick bill," which was passed by the legislature in 1884. This law made it a felony to brand a maverick, save under direction of an appointee of the stock association, and then with the letter M, as the property of the state, to be sold each April in advance of their gathering, to the highest bidder for cash, certified checks being required to accompany the bids for the estimated amount of the purchase. The money went to the state and was used in paying the expenses of the cattle round-up and inspection. The law was declared unconstitutional by many of the leading lawyers, and deemed to be in the interest of corporations with large holdings.

It was directly contrary to the education previously given the cowboys, and juries made up in whole or in part of old-timers naturally hesitated in the matter of declaring a man a thief for doing what the law-makers themselves had taught the people to do. Hence, there was some trouble in convicting men for appropriating mavericks, but when branded cattle were stolen and proofs made, convictions followed.

CHAPTER I. WAR ON THE RUSTLERS — THE HANGING OF JIM AVERILL AND CATTLE KATE, ON THE SWEETWATER.

There being a few reckless fellows in

various parts of the state who lived by the theft of cattle and horses, it was comparatively an easy matter to create the impression that the losses sustained by cattlemen were much greater than the facts supported. It was as easy to say that a hundred big steers had been taken as to tell the truth and say that one or two were missing, and that some one had undoubtedly stolen them. This report of wholesale stealing excited the sympathy of the people generally, and here was a point gained. So many cattle could not be stolen by the few known thieves; there must be hundreds engaged in the nefarious business. Of whom does this army of brand-burners consist, was a very natural question. Somebody answered, "The little stockman and settler." Very soon it seemed to be understood that the owners of large herds looked upon all the settlers and homeseekers as rustlers among the herds for mavericks (unbranded animals),

11

and the name "Rustler" was used as synonymous with settler. This free use of an offensive term created more or less bad blood and was a direct encouragement to the actually vicious, because they could commit more thefts and charge them to the settlers.

Keeping in mind the fact, stated in the introduction, that the settler was an eyesore to the ranchman, by reason of his fencing up the best lands, it may be seen that the latter was an interested spectator, if not an active promoter of the attaching of the disgraceful title of Rustler to all country homeseekers. In fact, public opinion has settled down to the belief that the corporation managers conceived the Rustler howl for the purpose of securing public sympathy for their future efforts to "run the settler out" by murder, assassination and incendiarism.

The first open and murderous attack made upon the settler by the cattlemen of the then territory, was in the summer of 1889, on the Sweetwater, in Carbon county. James Averill had taken a claim on the rich valley lands and opened a small store, where a postoffice had been established, with Averill as postmaster. Adjoining Averill's claim "Cattle Kate" (Ella Watson) had also taken a claim. These claims were in the center of a large section of country occupied by a cattle ranch, and the presence of the squatters, or settlers there were distasteful to the "Lord of the Manor." Averill sold whisky, but was a quiet, peaceably disposed person, with many friends among the cowboys and the settlers in the outlying districts. He was never accused of cattle stealing. Cattle Kate was a lewd woman and spent part of her time in an annex of Averill's house. She had a small pasture enclosed and gradually accumulated a bunch of young cattle, variously reported at from fifty to eighty head. These she had purchased from the cowboys and ranchmen. The large cattlemen charged that these cattle had been stolen from them by the cowboys and given to Cattle Kate in the way of business exchange; but no civil or criminal action was ever begun in the courts to prove these allegations.

Defying all forms of law, ten cattlemen rode up to Averill's store and with guns pointing at their victims, took Averill and the woman out of the house and hanged them until they were dead. There was known to be one young man present as a witness, and another party was reported to have been near enough to identify the lynchers. The boy was an invalid and was taken in charge by the cattlemen. He lingered some weeks and died—rumor strongly insisting, at the hands of his protectors, by the administration of a slow poison. The second party gave the list of those engaged in the tragedy and they were reported to the Carbon County Grand Jury. Meantime the informant was hunted like a wild beast, and as he failed to appear before the grand jury, and has never been seen or heard from since a few days after the hanging, the supposition is that he sleeps beneath the sod in some lonely mountain gorge where naught but the yelp of the passing wolf disturbs the solemnity of his last resting place. Or, perchance, this same howling beast picked the bones and left them to bleach on the barren hillside.

When the court convened and the grand jury was called no case was made against the little band of prominent citizens who had arrogated to themselves the power over life, and they were discharged. But the crime of taking two lives without a trial by jury had been committed just the same, and the disgrace of hanging a woman fastened upon the state. This incident greatly excited the people throughout the territory and widened the breach already opening between the ranchman and the settler.

On the other hand, the success of the "enterprise," and the failure to successfully prosecute the perpetrators of the outrage, gave special encouragement to the stock growers and they determined to "continue the good work."

CHAPTER II. THE HANGING OF WAGGONER NEAR NEWCASTLE—ATTACK UPON NATHAN D. CHAMPION AND ROSS GILBERTSON ON POWDER RIVER—BRUTAL AND COWARDLY MURDER OF JOHN A. TISDALE AND ORLEY E. JONES IN JOHNSON COUNTY.

Emboldened by exemption from

prosecution for the Sweetwater executions, the cattle ring determined to begin a systematic and indiscriminate slaughter of their supposed enemies. They had in their employ men of known recklessness and daring, and apparently the plan was to have these hired assassins begin on the eastern side of the state and pick off their men as they came to them. The first job was the hanging of Waggoner, a few miles from Newcastle, on the morning of June 4th, 1891.

Three men went to his house and with false papers took him under arrest. He was alone with his wife and two small children, so his friends were ignorant of his arrest; in fact, his wife supposed he had gone with friends and quietly awaited his return,

14

unsuspicious of foul play. The body was found on the 12th of June hanging to a tree in a gulch some miles away, since known as "Dead Man's Canon." When found the mustache had dropped from the flesh, the face was black, the hands pinnioned behind and decomposition rapidly doing its work.

Naturally great excitement prevailed in the community when the discovery of the body was made, and for a time there seemed a likeliehood of more trouble. The savage brutality characterising the act of leaving a human body hanging in the woods to be eaten by vultures or devoured by wolves was calculated to stir the blood of the average citizen. But the cattlemen's domination in the community proved superior to the resisting forces and the matter was dropped after a partial investigation, with no arrests made. Circumstances quite clearly pointed to certain men as the lynchers, but in Western parlance, they "had a pull," and no official action was taken.

Waggoner came to Wyoming from Nebraska and was engaged in the horse-raising business. His herd increased quite rapidly and the stockmen called him a rustler. This was never established and today there are many reputable people who declare that he was brave, kind-hearted, generous and a law-abiding citizen. His 1,000 head of horses have been virtually lost to the heirs by legal protection, but thus far none of them have been identified as "stolen."

Just before daylight on the morning of November 1st, 1891, four men entered the cabin of W. H. Hall, on Powder river, where Nathan D. Champion and Ross Gilbertson were living. As the door swung open it stood against the foot of the bunk occupied by Champion. With pistols pointed, one of the party said, "Give up; we have got you this time," and immediately fired at the body of Champion. The latter seized his revolvers from under his pillow and commenced shooting, whereupon the would-be murderers escaped from the house. The blood at the door, the gun, clothing and horses left near the cabin not only evidenced the fact of some effective shooting on the part of Champion, but gave identification as to the assaulters. Joe Elliott was arrested, charged with attempt to murder, and on a preliminary hearing put under $5,000 bonds. The witness having been killed or run out of the country, the case was finally dismissed.

Defeated in their attempt to kill Champion and Gilbertson, and getting the worst of the house-breaking plan, the stockmen naturally put their heads together to devise other methods of procedure. Bodily safety seemed to be a controlling idea in the new system of campaign, which proved to be that of ambushing. District Court met in Buffalo late in November, 1891, and business of one kind or another called in many of the country people. This would afford the desired opportunity to waylay their victims on the road going to or returning from the county seat. True to the well-matured plans, the killing began on the evening of the 28th of November.

Orley E. Jones, familiarly known as "Ranger Jones," a young man of 23 years, went to Buffalo to arrange for lumber to complete his house on his claim, expecting to get married as soon as the building was ready for occupancy. He started home on the afternoon of the 28th, driving two horses to a buckboard. At the crossing of Muddy creek, fifteen miles out from town, he was shot three times by some one in hiding under the bridge. The wagon was taken to a gully some distance from the road, the horses turned loose and Jones' body left in the buckboard, the murderer or murderers seeking safety in flight.

J. A. Tisdale, who lived sixty miles from Buffalo, had gone in to purchase winter supplies for his family and, after a few days' visit, started home on the evening of the 30th, spending the night at the Cross H. ranch, four miles out. Tisdale stated to friends in Buffalo that he had overheard Frank M. Canton tell Fred Hesse that he (Canton) would take care of Tisdale, and that he feared he would be killed on the road home. He was nervous and uneasy, and as a precaution bought a double-barrelled shotgun to carry. A local writer, speaking of this incident, says:

Tisdale still showed his uneasiness at the Cross H. ranch, and that night had the window blinds all closed and told one of the boys there that he thought the cowmen were going to kill him. He started the next morning on his journey home. Three miles on his murderer was lying in a gulch within twenty feet of the road, waiting for his victim to approach. Slowly but surely Tisdale, with his heavy load, was going to meet his death at the hands of the cowardly fiend. He approached, passed, and when twenty-five feet by, the murderer's rifle belched forth its deadly contents. The first shot, from appearances, struck the handle of his six-shooter, which he had under his coat on the left side, and glanced off. He had evidently tried to cock and shoot his shotgun then, for one of the cartridges was indented slightly, as though he had drawn the hammer back part way, and it had then slipped from his thumb, he having received a death shot in the side, before he had time to fully cock it, and the poor fellow fell back on his load shot to death.

To avoid immediate discovery the wagon and team were driven half a mile below, the horses shot and the wagon and dead man left out of sight from the road. But Charles Basch, approaching from the south on horseback, had witnessed at least a part of the murderous deed, and he rode to Buffalo and gave notice of same. Basch charged Frank M. Canton with being the murderer. Sheriff Angus sent a deputy and a small posse after the body and it was taken to town. The village was full of country people, and excitement ran high. About the time of the arrival of Tisdale's body Jones' brother reached town, having grown nervous over his non-appearance. A searching party was quickly organized and in the evening the body of Ranger Jones was discovered in a gully near the crossing of the Muddy, as detailed above, having lain in the buckboard for three days. Here was cause for still greater excitement, but the officers of the law had no trouble in preserving order.

Charles Basch having accused Frank M. Canton with the murder of Tisdale, it was generally believed that he also ambushed and murdered Jones, though a few persons thought Fred Hesse was the guilty party taking the cue from Tisdale's remark that he had overheard Canton tell Hesse that he would "take care of Tisdale," thus implying that that was his share of the bloody work, and that others were to do their share.

Canton was arrested and given a preliminary hearing before Justice of the Peace Parmalee. Two days were spent in the trial, when the accused was released.

The people freely charged the court with corruption and declared the evidence ample to justify the placing of the prisoner behind the bars without bail. Only the presence of cool heads in the community prevented the wrecking of vengeance upon Canton and some of his sympathizers. Canton and Hesse left the state in a few days. Some time later new and material evidence was found and a new information was filed. Canton was in the state of Illinois, and Governor Barber was asked to issue a requisition for his return. This request the governor refused. In March, 1892, Canton returned to Cheyenne to join the invaders, and the papers were served upon him. Laramie City being in the same judicial district with Buffalo, Canton was taken before Judge Blake in chambers, and given a hearing. He was held in bonds of $30,000, for which sum the following named persons qualified as sureties, the bond bearing date of April 4th, 1892:

Hubert E. Teschemacher, Wm. C. Irvine, E. S. Rouse Boughton, Fred G. S. Hesse, Lafayette H. Parker, A. R. Powers, Joseph G. Pratt, Elias W. Whitcomb, Arthur B. Clarke, John N. Tisdale, David R. Tisdale, James W. Hammond, Charles S. Ford, Henry W. Davis, George P. Bissell, William E. Guthrie, Ralph M. Friend, George W. Baxter, Hiram B. Ijams, Frank H. Laberteaux and Ranslaer S. Van Tassell.

These cowardly shootings in the back from places of safety completed a list of dead at the hands of the cattle barons as follows: Jim Averill, Ella Watson, Tom Waggoner, O. E. Jones, and J. A. Tisdale, to say nothing of the attempts to murder, and yet they went unwhipped of justice, to plan and execute other forms of oppression and other methods of murder. No wonder the people of the state everywhere looked upon the cattlemen as being arrayed against them and as the enemies of true progress and development in the commonwealth. The eyes of the masses were opened to the situation.

CHAPTER III. ORGANIZING THE INVASION — THE WYOMING STOCK GROWERS' ASSOCIATION AS A PROMOTER—CHEYENNE THE RENDEZVOUS OF THE PLOTTERS — ACTING GOVERNOR AMOS W. BARBER PREPARING THE WAY FOR THE INVADERS.

The invasion of the state of Wyoming

by a band of cutthroats and hired assassins in April, 1892, was the crowning infamy of the ages. Nothing so cold-blooded, so brutal, so bold and yet so cowardly was ever before recorded in the annals of the world's history. The results proved disastrous to the outlaws themselves and cast a shadow upon the name of the state that will require a decade of years to dissipate by the sunlight of a continuous prosperity. The crime was so great that the lapse of years will only tend to magnify it in the minds of all readers of Wyoming history. In this case the sins of men will live after them. The audacity, the foolhardiness, of the gang of desperadoes was such that a study of how it was planned and upon what they relied for success, seems a necessity in order to convey to the mind of the reader the impression that the whole story is not a fiction, the work of an overwrought imagination. Hence, this stopping by the way to illustrate the various steps taken.

It is believed that early in the year 1891 it was determined by the stockmen to terrorize the ranchmen and rustlers of the northern part of the state and drive them from the ranges. How, it mattered not. H. B. Ijams, secretary of the Board of Livestock Commissioners, takes to himself credit for suggesting to the board the idea of seizing the cattle shipped to market by such persons as the stockmen saw proper to class as "rustlers," have the money sent to him as secretary of the board, in Cheyenne, and force the shippers to make a pilgrimage to the capitol to prove their property. It was believed that this would so embarrass and cripple the little fellows that they would go out of the business. Thousands of cattle were so seized, and considerable money thus obtained yet remains tied up in the hands of the commission.

In January, 1891, the Legislature passed an act creating the "Board of Livestock Commissioners of Wyoming." The board consists of three members, and employs a secretary.

Following are the sections that, in the opinion of Mr. Ijams, justify the action taken as above indicated:

Sec. 13. The Board of Livestock Commissioners shall exercise a general supervision over, and so far as may be, protect the livestock interests of the state from theft and disease, and shall recommend from time to time such legislation as in their judgment will foster said industry.

Sec. 17. Said Board of Livestock Commissioners is hereby authorized and it is made its duty to appoint such stock inspectors as it may deem necessary for the better protection of the livestock interests of the state, and to distribute them at such points or places within or without the state as will in their judgment most effectually prevent the violation of any and all laws of the state for the protection of stock.

Sec. 26. It shall be the duty of all persons shipping estrays at once upon the sale thereof to remit to the secretary of the livestock commission the proceeds received for each and every estray, the ownership of which shall be unknown to the inspector to whom a receipt for the same was given. If any inspector shall at any time sell an estray shipped from this state, he shall immediately remit the proceeds thereof to the secretary of the livestock commission.

Sec. 29. The secretary of the livestock commission upon satisfactory proof of the ownership of any estray sold as above provided, and for which he has received the money, shall pay such owner the amount received from the sale of such estray or estrays; Provided, That such ownership shall be proven within one year after the publication of the notice of sale of said estray or estrays, as above provided. Proof of the ownership shall be by affidavit of the owner with at least one credible corroborating witness.

Just where the extra judicial power conferred upon the board is given is difficult to see in the above. Yet it has been freely exercised.

This plan, while it worked a great hardship upon many innocent people, did not deter the settlers from attempting to raise and ship cattle to market. Failing in this, more heroic methods were adopted, as delineated in Chapter II. Still unsuccessful in gaining control of the rich valleys of the north a large number of prominent stockmen met in Cheyenne in the early winter of 1891-2 and presumably agreed upon the invasion as later planned in detail.

Money was a prime necessity and a subscription paper was circulated among all the stockmen of the state, who were believed to be in sympathy with the movement, and it is said by some who saw the list that nearly a hundred thousand dollars was subscribed to this "Extermination Fund," if we may coin an expression to fit. The cash being provided for, the next thing in order was to gather in the leaders and see upon what ground they stood. True, a good many ranchmen refused to contribute and be a party to the proposed outrage, but enough, in the opinion of the inner circle of plotters, had been committed to force the others into line.

The three members of the Wyoming Board of Livestock Commissioners, J. W. Hammond, W. C. Irvine and Charles Hecht, state officers, were in the city most of the winter. Frank Walcott, of Glenrock, came in about, or soon after the holidays, and several other leading stock raisers from various parts of the state and from the East, were frequently seen in the city. These, in connection with several cattlemen domiciled in Cheyenne, made a large list of interested parties to work for a common end.

Ex-Governor Baxter's office, in the Commercial Block, seemed to be the invasion incubator, for there Walcott and Irvine, the first and second in command of the cutthroat army, generally were to be found in consultation "over private business," as the man in the outer office was wont to explain to callers.

Knowing that their contemplated action was in direct and flagrant opposition to all law and an over-riding of the constitution of the state, it was necessary to ascertain how those in authority would look upon the matter. Acting Governor Barber, as executive of the civil government and commander-in-chief of the state militia, was the first man to look after. During the months of February and March the Governor and the stockmen were almost inseparable. Irvine, Walcott, Baxter, Ijams, Hammond and Hay seemed each to be a twin brother of the executive, and at his office, adjoining the Cheyenne Club House, the passerby in the night could almost always see one or more of these people closeted with or going into the governor's place. That they captured him, body and soul, his later official acts and his refusal to act abundantly testify. The path from Baxter's office to the acting governor's dormitory might appropriately be termed the trail of blood.

Having made "medicine" with the governor, friendly relations were to be created with the military at Fort D. A. Russell. That these efforts were in a measure successful is evidenced by the capture of government tents with the invading hosts, supposed to have been loaned to them by some of the post officers.

Presumably the United States Senators, Warren and Carey, needed no coaching. Both were leading stock growers, and general rumor credits Carey with being a contributor to the working fund of $1,000 in cash and other valuable considerations.

Other Senators and men high in the nation's councils are believed to have been led into approval of the diabolical scheme by misrepresentation and fraud.

Dropping back to the state officials, their action after the collapse of the murderous raid led the people generally to believe that many of them not only knew of the plans laid, but actually gave encouragement to their carrying out.

Being reasonably assured of the official support of the state authorities and important outside aid, as early as January, 1892, a systematic effort was made to create public sentiment favorable to their hellish work, through the press outside of the state. During the holiday season a long article appeared in the Washington Star abusing the people of Johnson county, classing them as rustlers and bad men generally. It made a great story out of the wrongs suffered by the cattlemen, and was evidently inspired by some person informed as to what the spring months would usher in on the plains of Northern Wyoming. Omaha, Chicago, New York and Philadelphia papers also contained frequent articles calculated to make their readers believe that a reign of terror existed in half a dozen counties in the state that could only be overcome by a resort to arms, especially as all the court and peace officers of these counties were said to be open and avowed rustlers or acknowledged sympathizers therewith. This class of reading matter was uncommon for the papers publishing it, and could not have appeared so uniform in character and even in dates without some inspiring hand behind it. The only rational conclusion, therefore, is that the invader managers had a literary bureau charged with the duty of creating a public sentiment in the land to which they could point as a moral backing of their future developments. This work was carried down to the day of entering the field, and even after the capture of the outfit. For weeks before the start the Denver papers fairly bristled with bloodcurdling stories of the outrages committed by the desperate homeseekers north of the Platte river against the poor cattle kings.

These preliminary arrangements had all been so easily and successfully worked that the stockmen seemingly actually believed they could capture the state, run its country people over the border and return to the conditions present when there was no man in all the north country save the festive cowboy and he a law unto himself. As evidence that they had arrived at this frame of mind, the following interviews with H. B. Ijam and

George W. Baxter, of Cheyenne, given in Denver, Colorado, while the expedition was in the north, are cited. The first is copied from the Cheyenne Daily Tribune, one of the invaders most trusted organs, of date April 12, 1892, and we give it as it appeared in that delectable sheet, head lines and all. It shows very clearly how the ex-governor felt at that time, and what his hopes were founded upon. It is good reading at this late date:

WIPE THEM OUT

All Honest Citizens Are in Hopes That the Cattlemen Will Exterminate the Rustlers — Governor Baxter Is Interviewed — What Northern Cattlemen Have to Say About the Warfare—Other Questions Discussed.

DENVER, April 12.—Ex-Governor Baxter of Wyoming and Judd Brush of Greeley, president of the Cattle Growers' Association, are in the city, in company with a number of prominent cattlemen of this state and Wyoming. A member of the party, in speaking of troubles in Wyoming, said: "The sympathies of nine-tenths of the people of Wyoming are with the cattle owners. I do not know to what extent the people of Colorado are informed as to the points at issue in the fight which is now fairly under way, but from what I have learned I am willing to give all the assistance possible to any body of men which will attempt to exterminate the rustlers.

"The latter have terrorized whole communities for years and practically control the actions of officials in several counties of the state. The cattlemen who have gone into the state at the head of the fighters whom they can trust, are men who were driven off the ranges by the rustlers. Many of these men saved their lives only by escaping on fast ponies under cover of darkness. The time has come when they must quit the state altogether or make a fight to the death. The party was organized quietly in this city, as it was felt that the preliminary arrangements could not be safely made in Wyoming, so widespread is the influence of the rustlers."

"Is there no other way by which the interests of the cattlemen could be protected?"

"Absolutely none. The courts have been appealed to time after time, in vain. Grand juries refused to indict the cattle thieves, although in many cases the rustlers appeared before the jury and acknowledged their guilt. It is simply a battle for existence on the part of the cattle owners in half a dozen counties. They must maintain their positions with rifles or let the robbers have full sway. I have been told of instances where the rustlers served notice on merchants, saying that they must keep quiet or suffer condign punishment."

The day before the above quoted interview H. B. Ijams, secretary of the Wyoming Board of Livestock Commissioners, was in Denver, and a Republican reporter interviewed him at length. From his statements we reproduce the following extract:

I do not believe any of these reports, he said, of conflicts having taken place. I think that all these dispatches are inspired by the rustlers and their sympathizers. There are newspapers of Wyoming which have always advocated the cause of the thieves and they are still at work fixing up these reports. The rustlers have charge of the wires and I am waiting now for the time when our men can get hold of them. So while I am pretty much in the dark I am certain that the true situation of things has not been told.

A SURGEON WITH THE INVADERS

One thing I know cannot be true. The dispatches say that a wounded man was brought into Buffalo who was supposed to be one of our invaders. That is absurd. A good surgeon, with everything which he might need, is with the invaders, and if anybody is hurt he is taken care of in the camp. They are well provided with everything that may be needed. And I want to emphasize strongly the character of the invading party. There are about sixty good men, and of that number twenty especially are among the best citizens of the whole state. They are men who have been driven out of Johnson county by the gang of rustlers, and they are going back for—well, "retribution" is a good word.

FIGHTING FOR HOME AND PROPERTY

They are fighting for life, home and property, and I want to predict that the rustlers will be wiped out. With the aid of Sheriff Angus, the rustlers cannot muster as many men by far as our party will have in the field very soon. As for the militia, I fancy that most of them are now with one party or the other. The company at Buffalo will pretty certainly stick to the rustlers. The "TA" ranch, where the fight is said to have occurred, is owned by Dr. Harris of Laramie City and his foreman is one of the leaders of the invading party.

EXPLAINING DISPATCHES

Now I think I can explain some of the vague dispatches. Men come in to Casper and Cheyenne and other towns with stories of what they have seen or heard, when they have no foundation for such tales. Before I left Cheyenne a man came in from the west and began to tell how he had met "our" party well out on our journey. I questioned him pretty closely and knowing just exactly the make-up of our party, it soon proved that his story was an entire fabrication. So it is with the most of the messengers from the seat of war. There may have been a fight or several of them, but I doubt it. Our party is not going at things hastily, and when we do hear reliable news, it will be of a very decided nature.

It is useless for me to go into a history of this trouble and the conditions leading up to it. The Republican has given the account very accurately and completely. All we need now is news, news.

Vague rumors of disaster to the cattlemen had reached the press and these two valiant long-range fighters, taken by surprise, unbosomed themselves, thus giving a clear insight to the public of the faith of the consitution wreckers then on the gory field of battle, and the camp followers engaged in feeling and trying to regulate the public pulse.

Another thing that gave hope was the belief that they had fully enlisted the sympathy of the president of the United States in their behalf. On the 17th of April the following telegram was sent from Paris, Texas, to the San Francisco Chronicle and published generally throughout the country:

About two weeks ago eleven men, who had for years been acting as either United States deputy marshals or deputy sheriffs, left here rather mysteriously, and it was given out that they had gone West to enter the cattle business. They belong to the party that was rounded up by the troops and rustlers and taken to Fort McKinney. It turned out that they were sent to Wyoming by the United States government to help the big ranchmen protect themselves from the raids of the rustlers. The large cattlemen, it is said, appealed to President Harrison for protection, and offered to pay for men who would come and aid them in maintaining what they considered their rights. The president requested the marshals of the Eastern, Western and Northern districts of Texas to go to Wyoming at once, and a party of forty-three was organized. It is said that they took oaths as Pinkerton detectives.

While it is probably not true that the president had any conception of the depth of villainy to which the treason plotters were stooping, it has been generally understood that his consent to a transfer of deputy marshal from the South to Wyoming had been secured. That an effort was made to gather up a large number of these Southern deputies by the agents of the invaders is known, and the braggadocio with which Ijams speaks in the above quotation when he says: "Angus and the rustlers cannot muster as many men by far as our party will have in the field very soon," indicates that recruits were expected from this direction. The circumstances and conditions strongly point to some kind of an understanding with the United States Marshal's office at Washington, if not with a higher power.

It is evident, also, from the tone of the Baxter-Ijams interviews given above that they expected many recruits from Denver, and were in that city to aid in forwarding a second battalion to the front. Squads were promised from Casper, Douglas and Newcastle, and it is known that a case of guns was shipped to Douglas, addressed to Acting Governor Barber about that time, and later shipped to Cheyenne, without being opened, presumably because the volunteers were all on the other side. Buffalo was booked for a hundred men, and stragglers were to come in from the Big Horn and other places. But none of these auxiliaries materialized. Baxter's "nine-tenths of the people of Wyoming" were found to be in sympathy with the people and against "the cattle owners."

All of these promises to aid, and the splendid detail of plans laid, however, led Baxter to boastingly say to the Denver interviewer, "I am willing to give all the assistance possible to any body of men which will attempt to exterminate the rustlers." This promised assistance did not seem to arouse the common herd of Denver to the enlisting point, notwithstanding the liberal terms of $5 a day and $50 for each and every scalp taken by any of the force. (See Downing's confession in the appendix).

As evidence of complicity between Wyoming's acting governor and the invaders it is in order to present the following transcript from the books of the Adjutant General's office:

Cheyenne, Wyo., March 23, 1892.

General Order No. 4.

Colonel De Forest Richards, Commanding First Regiment, Wyoming National Guards:

Sir—Colonel De Forest Richards, commanding First Regiment Infantry, Wyoming National Guards, is hereby directed to instruct his company commanders that they shall obey only such orders to assemble their commands as may be received from these headquarters, to assist the civil authorities in the preservation or enforcement of the laws of the state of Wyoming.

By order of the Governor and Commander-in-Chief.
    (Signed)   FRANK STITZER,
                                                                          Adjutant General.

In order to show that the above order is in direct violation of
the laws of Wyoming the following copy of Section 33, Chapter
85, Session Laws, 1890, is given:

Sec. 33.   Whenever in any county there is tumult, riot, mob or any
body of men acting together with intent to commit a felony, or to do or
offer violence to person or property, or by force or violence to break
or resist the laws of the territory, or in case of an Indian outbreak, and
the civil authorities are unable to suppress the same, or there is reasonable apprehension thereof, the governor or sheriff of the county, or the
mayor or judge, during the absence of the governor, may issue his call
to the commanding officer of any regiment, battalion, company, troop
or battery, to order his command, or any part thereof, describing the
same, to be and appear at a time and place therein specified to act in aid
of the civil authority.

Why should Amos W. Barber, acting governor, violate this
plainly written statute? Why should he, by an official act, over-
ride the law and transfer the power to call out the militia from
the civil to the military branch of the state government? It was a
very strange proceeding. There is but one explanation possible
—it was a necessary safeguard to the invaders. With that law
in force the moment a band of invaders crossed the line of Converse or Johnson counties the respective sheriffs would call out
the company and contest their advance. This would be a menace
to the cattlemen. There was a strong company at Douglas and
one at Buffalo. Malcomb Campbell of Converse county, and
W. G. Angus of Johnson, were known to be men who would act
promptly in an emergency, and shape their action to the interest
of the people. The military must be withdrawn from their call.
This order was made on the 23rd day of March, and on April 5th
the cattlemen's forces moved on Johnson county—a "mob, or
body of men acting together with intent to offer violence to person or property," in the county; but the hands of the sheriff
were tied, so far as the authority to call out the military was
concerned. Do you see how nicely the order fit the case? Can
any fair-minded reader fail to realize that general order No. 4

was issued for the protection of the cattlemen while engaged in their bloody work—to render the settlers of Johnson county helpless in the hands of a gang of men supposed to be large enough in numbers to burn and loot the premises of the lone settlers on the public domain?

The constitution of the state of Wyoming contains the following distinct and easily understood utterance:

Article No. XIX.—Police Powers.—Section 1. No armed police force, or detective agency, or armed body, or unarmed body of men, shall ever be brought into this state for the suppression of domestic violence, except upon the application of the Legislature or executive, when the Legislature cannot be convened.

Under the above section of the constitution the duty of the governor is clearly manifest in the emergency of an invasion of the state. Amos W. Barber was acting governor of Wyoming on the 5th day of April, 1892, when an armed body of men came on a special train from Denver, and after stopping for a time in Cheyenne, rolled away on another special train made up at the city depot and stockyards for the northern part of the state, on murder and arson bent. His closest personal friends with whom he had been in intercourse most of the day, joined the gang at the depot, and it was simply impossible, under the circumstances, for him not to have known of the violation of the constitution being perpetrated. The governor is commander-in-chief of the state troops, yet he folded his arms and allowed the hired army to move on the unsuspecting settlers while they were plowing for their spring crops and endeavoring to provide for the wants of wives and children.

But were it possible not to understand the conditions present at that time, the following day everybody knew what had happened and an intercepting order could have been sent and the troops ordered out. This was not done. When asked why, he replied that he had no official knowledge of the violation of the constitution and could not act on simple hearsay. Waiting for the barn to burn before the water was turned on.

In order that the acting governor may not be misrepresented, the following clipping is taken from the Cheyenne Leader of April 8th, 1892:

Governor Barber was seen yesterday and asked if he had taken any action with reference to the armed body of men which entered and passed through the state on Tuesday evening.

"I have not," he replied. "The matter has not been brought to my attention officially. I only know of the matter through newspaper reports which, as you know," he added with a smile, "are somewhat conflicting on the subject."

"Do you intend to take any official notice of the matter?"

"As soon as I have learned the facts I will take such steps as I may deem necessary. I was more interested in the statement from Douglas published in the Leader yesterday than anything else. It was to the effect that the militia could hereafter be only ordered out by the commander-in-chief. This matter has been under consideration ever since the last Legislature adjourned. Previous to that under certain circumstances judges, sheriffs or mayors could call out the militia. This was changed by the last Legislature so that this power rests exclusively with the governor. During my absence from the state I was much worried that something of this sort would be done. The idea of the order was to make it plain that the militia could only be ordered out by the governor, as no one else now has that authority. The order was issued over a month ago."

The reader can compare the law quoted above, which was then and is now in force, with Barber's statement, and draw his own conclusions as to exclusive power resting with the governor. Besides, if the law conferred no authority upon "judges, sheriffs and mayors," why issue an order to prevent the exercise of power not possessed? The peculiar exigencies of the case seemed to demand it — namely, the preservation of the proposed invaders.

Another circumstance that confirms the belief in the mind of the general public that the governor had a guilty knowledge of the proposed invasion is the fact that Charles B. Penrose was employed as surgeon to the invaders and accompanied them for a time on their raid. When captured he had in his possession a case of surgical instruments belonging to Governor Barber, and no one will accuse him of stealing them—they must have been loaned to him for use, and loaned by their owner. Dr. Penrose was a close personal friend of the governor, and was in Cheyenne as his guest at the time of the start. Is it reasonable to suppose that this stranger would accept so responsible a position as surgeon general of an invading army without consulting his old college chum with whom he was in daily contact?

Having smoothed the way of the transgressors to the satisfaction of themselves, the steering committee began to look around for fighting material. To meet on anything like equal footing the hardy pioneers who had braved all the dangers of frontier life required men of nerve, practical experience and good horsemanship. Texas and the Southwest was the most inviting field, so a number of special agents were sent there to open recruiting stations. The wages offered were flattering, and to a certain class of reckless men sufficient inducement to undertake the hazardous job. Fortunately for the information of the public George Dunning, one of the hired men, made a confession, under oath, and told the terms upon which all of the men were recruited. These were $5 a day and all expenses paid, including a mount of horses, pistols and rifle. In addition, each man of the command was to receive $50 for each and every man killed by the mob. George W. Baxter, R. M. Allen, Frank M. Canton, Tom Smith and a few others are reported as the recruiting agents sent to the Southwest, while it is known that H. B. Ijams went on the same mission to Idaho. The work of enlisting was a little slow, for brave, honorable men hesitated when given to understand exactly what was expected of them. Going to war in the regular way, when patriotism and duty calls, is one thing—going to fight for a set of corporation cormorants against settlers on the public domain simply for the money there is in it, is quite another. However, with the long list of ex-deputy marshals and thoughtless cowboys between the piney woods of Texas and the Rio Grande, the agents of the cattlemen believed they had secured sufficient force to be effective in connection with the large number of volunteers promised from Wyoming and adjoining sections.

So the men were ordered to report at Denver, Colorado, the 1st of April, 1892, where they were to be met by a committee, after the annual meeting of the Wyoming Stock Growers' Association, on the 4th. The association meeting was attended by

many leading cattle raisers from all over the state, and while
nothing is known by the public as to what its secret actions were,
it is believed that the work of the several special committees
was approved and the general plan of the campaign adopted.
Results immediately following force the above conclusion.

Before adjournment on the 4th, the following resolution was
introduced by W. E. Guthrie and passed by a unanimous vote:

Whereas, The cattle interests of this state have been seriously
jeopardized by thieves and outlaws; and

Whereas, Many herds are leaving this state to seek protection elsewhere; be it

Resolved, That the Wyoming Stock Growers' Association appreciates
and endorses the able and fearless manner in which the Board of Livestock Commissioners have attempted to guard the interests of honest
cattle owners in the state, acting as they have without compensation or
reward, and solely for the general good and prosperity of the state; be
it further

Resolved, That we believe all money now withheld by such board to
be the proceeds of stolen cattle, and that we commend their cause in
retaining the same until proof of ownership shall be made.

This is a direct reversal of all law and practice—branding
men as thieves and then requiring them to prove themselves
honest, instead of counting them honest until proven to be dis-
honest. It was an approval of the idea of the invasion—taking
the law into their own hands, or rising superior to the law and
declaring that they "were a law unto themselves."

The Idaho contingent was ordered to report at Cheyenne,
and a squad was expected to be at Casper. About twenty-five
men were gathered at Cheyenne, and all day during the 5th the
work of preparation was going on. Guns and pistols were purchased by the score and ammunition was carted out by wagon
loads. Rolls of blankets were shipped, and altogether it was a
busy day in the Capitol City.

The plan of the campaign, it is believed, was to go direct to
Buffalo, kill Sheriff Angus and his deputies and there be re-
enforced with a large number of co-workers, when they would
capture the town, kill twenty or thirty citizens and then raid the
settlements in the county, killing or driving out several hundred

more, thus getting rid of all their enemies. After satiating themselves with the blood of Johnson county's citizens, they undoubtedly expected to make detours into Natrona, Converse and Weston counties, where they had dead lists in the hands of the mob, covering many settlers and some business men in each county. Spotters were already in each county locating the men to be killed, and apparently they anticipated a regular picnic in their work of death. One leading idea seemed to be that a reign of terror would at once be brought about and that hundreds of settlers would gather up their families and fly for safety before the approach of the crimson-handed slayers. To prevent the sending of news by wire in advance of the cutthroat band, men had been posted along the telegraph line leading north with instructions to cut the wires, and leave the communities in ignorance of their approaching danger.

CHAPTER IV. THIRTY HIRED ASSASSINS AND TWENTY REPRESENTATIVE STOCKMEN LEAVE CHEYENNE TO MURDER, BURN AND DESTROY—THE FINAL PREPARATIONS AND THE START — ARRIVAL AT CASPER AND DEPARTURE, MOUNTED, ACROSS THE COUNTRY.

Monday and Tuesday, April 4th and

5th, 1892, will always be remembered as red letter days in the criminal history of Cheyenne, the capitol city of Wyoming, the baby state of the American Union. Leading members of the Wyoming Stockgrowers' Association were engaged on these two days branding a bunch of seventy odd picked and highly fed horses with the unrecorded, or "Maverick" brand A on the left shoulder, loading them in cars, and putting in other cars saddles, harness, tents, ammunition, giant powder, provisions, etc. Late in the afternoon of the 5th a special train came in from Denver, Colorado, carrying the southern contingent of hired murderers. Stopping for an hour in the east end of the switching yards, the cars were then taken across the Crow creek bridge to the stockyards, where the stock and baggage cars, already loaded, were attached, and at 6 o'clock the start was made for Casper, two hundred miles to the northwest. The mob consisted of somewhere between fifty and sixty men, divided about equally between hired helpers from the South and Wyoming citizens. These latter were in the proportion of about two stockmen to one hired man. Each person was armed with a brace of pistols and a Winchester rifle.

The leaders were anxious for a start at their bloody work, Major Walcott, in command, as a parting salute, saying to the railroad superintendent, "Hurry up; put us at Casper and we will do the rest."

The track was clear and a fast run was made to Casper, that point being reached three or four hours before daylight the next morning. The train was stopped at the stockyards, some distance outside of the town, and before sunrise the wagons were loaded, the horsemen mounted, and the cavalcade on the move across the open prairie, following the guides who had been summoned to be in waiting.

Before reaching Casper a stop was made at the Fort Fetterman stockyards, where Ed David, the general range manager for Senator Carey, was taken aboard with two well caparisoned saddle horses, blankets, guns, etc. But there was heaps of trouble on young David's mind. He had promised, and was expected to go on the raid. Serious consideration of the matter, however, had caused him to reconsider and cancel his engagement. Asked for his reason he stated that as Carey's foreman, if he went on the trip, it would connect the United States senator directly with the invasion and destroy his future political advancement, a thing not to be tolerated for a moment. There was a good deal of back talk on the part of the commanding officers, but it was finally agreed that David should give his horses and outfit to a man who had been hired to cut the telegraph wires, this man joining the band and David taking his place as the official wire-cutter of the expedition. The hired man accompanied the gang and the telegraph wires were cut—presumably by Ed David in accordance with his promise so to do. (This information comes under oath, and is reliable.)

There was a little music on the train as it rolled away, that will probably never reach the ear of the public in its sweetest tones. Several of our "best citizens" had pledged themselves to be of the party, and had gone so far as to purchase their outfits, but as the hour of departure drew near and the possibilities and realities of the campaign presented themselves, the spotless "white feather" lured them away from their professed allegiance to the cause, and they were—not on the train. The discussion of why these bovine worshippers were not present is reported as being more forcible than elegant, and yet withal exceedingly musical in its rythmic changes.

Seven miles out the invaders camped for breakfast. The balance of that day and the following were consumed in the march to Tisdale's ranch, forty odd miles from Casper. Two or three men were met on the road and forced to turn back and travel for hours. Then they were permitted to go their way on a promise of secrecy as to having met any force of men. Friends of the outfit at Casper and Douglas had been instructed to give out the information, should the mob be discovered and suspicions be aroused, that the passing men were a crowd of railroad surveyors, going to locate and hold a pass in the mountains. Major Walcott was supposed to be in command of the forces, with Canton as captain of the Wyoming men and Tom Smith over the Texans.

Just before reaching Tisdale's ranch Mike Shonsy, foreman of the Western Union Beef Company, rode up to the advancing column with the information that there were rustlers in the neighboring ranch, and after consultation among the leaders of the band that night, a change of route and plan was agreed upon.

CHAPTER V. COWARDLY ATTACK UPON THE K. C. RANCH — FLIGHT OF JACK FLAGG UNDER FIRE — CAPTURE OF THE TRAPPERS JONES AND WALKER — SHOOTING OF RAY — BURNING OF THE RANCH HOUSE — ATTEMPTED FLIGHT AND KILLING OF NATE CHAMPION — CHAMPION'S DIARY.

As indicated in the last chapter, the

information brought by Shonsy to the effect that there were rustlers at Nolan's K. C. ranch, on the North fork of Powder river, changed the route of the invaders. Friday, the 8th, was spent at Tisdale's, waiting for the supply wagons to come up. In the afternoon Shonsy, in charge of a squad, was sent to reconnoitre, the balance of the party following after nightfall. The design was to reach the ranch before daylight and blow up the house with dynamite, thus destroying all who chanced to be in the building. But daylight had broken when they reached the place and safety forbade too near approach to the dwelling, where "dead shots" might get the drop. So they concealed themselves in the stable, along the creek, that nearly surrounded the house, and in the brush of the ravine on the side opposite the creek. Having the premises completely surrounded and being themselves concealed, the besiegers waited the appearance of the inmates, expecting to shoot them down as they came out. Seeing a traveler's wagon in the yard, the suspicion was raised in the minds of the leaders that possibly some of their friends might be in the house, and orders were given "await orders" before shooting.

Presently a man came out with a bucket and walked down to the creek. He was captured and concealed behind the creek bank. Another man came from the house after a time and walked to the stable. He was captured and held. These men proved to be Jones and Walker, two trappers who had stopped over night at the ranch. In a little while Nick Ray came out of the house and walked several steps from the door when he was shot and felled to the ground. Champion rushed to the door, gun in hand, and poured a volley at the beseigers, all the time a hot fire being directed at him. He closed the door and evidently watched from the window whence he could see that his friend Ray was slowly crawling toward the door. When Ray was close to the step, Champion opened the door, sent another volley toward the stable and the creek, then laid down his gun and, with bullets thick as hail flying about him, stepped out and dragged his friend into the house.

A regular fusilade was kept up upon the house until the middle of the afternoon, and a good many shots were fired from the house. It is understood that several of Champion's shots took effect in the fleshy part of the assaillants, but none of them were dangerously hurt. About 3 o'clock in the afternoon Jack Flagg, on horseback, and his stepson came along the road and approached within a few rods of the mob, the men being concealed. This part of the day's doings has been told by Mr. Flagg in a newspaper article and is here reproduced as the best authority available. He says:

The morning of the 9th I started from my ranch, eighteen miles above on the river, to go to Douglas. I was on horseback, and my stepson, a boy 17 years of age, started with me to go to the Powder river crossing. He was driving two horses and had only the running gear of a 3 1-4 wagon. We got to the K. C. ranch about 2:30 p. m. I was riding about fifty yards behind the wagon. We could not see the stable, behind which the murderers were concealed, until we were within seventy-five yards of it. When the wagon hove in sight the murderers jumped up and commanded the boy to halt, but he urged up his horses and drove for the bridge. When they saw he would not stop, one of them took aim on the corner of the fence and fired at him. The shot missed him and scared his team, which stampeded across the bridge and on up the road.

There were twenty men behind the stable, and seven came up on horseback, three from one side of the road and four from the other and closed in behind me. When the men behind the stable saw me, they began to jump for their guns, which were leaning against the fence, and called on me to stop and throw up my hands. I did not comply with their order, but kept straight for the bridge. When I got to the nearest point to them—forty-seven steps—a man whom I recognized as Ford, stepped from the crowd and, taking deliberate aim at me with his Winchester, fired. Then they all commenced firing. I threw myself on the side of my horse and made a run for it. The seven horsemen followed me. When I overtook my wagon, which had my rifle on it, I told my boy to hand it to me, which he did; I then told him to stop and cut one of the horses loose and mount him. The seven horsemen were following me, and when I stopped, were 350 yards behind, but as soon as they saw I had a rifle, they stopped. I only had three cartridges for my rifle, and did not want to fire one of them, unless they came closer, which they did not seem inclined to do.

The escape of Flagg and his stepson was a sore trial to the banditti, as it made the giving of a general alarm to the settlers a certainty and in consequence gave promise of an uprising of the whole people in arms against their common enemies. Time was precious, and no more could be wasted on the besieged. The wagon left in the road was run down to the barn, loaded with hay and pitch pine wood, then backed up against the window of the house, Dunning says, by Major Walcott, A. B. Clark, John Tisdale, Tom Smith and James Dudley. A torch was applied and in a moment the building was a mass of flames.

Champion ran out at the south end of the house, gun in hand. A hundred shots were fired at him without effect, and no doubt he thought escape was possible. But as he approached the ravine two hundred yards from the house, a dozen men fired from the brush simultaneously. Even these whistling missiles of death passed him by and he raised his gun to reply. Before he could shoot a second volley belched forth from the hidden foes and brave Champion fell—hero in the hearts of all his neighbors. Many of the assassins must have fired repeatedly into his dead body before daring to approach it, for on being prepared for burial, twenty-eight bullets were found to have pierced him. Eye-witnesses differ slightly in their narratives of this exciting scene, but from a comparison of statements the above is believed to be a correct, though short summing up of the facts. For variety, and in order that there may lodge no charge of prejudice, the following account, from the pen of Sam T. Clover, correspondent of the Chicago Herald, who was with the regulators from the start until after the K. C. massacre, is given. Clover being in constant association with the free-booters was naturally looking through the colored glasses they had prepared for him, though no doubt trying to be impartial. He says:

The roof of the cabin was the first to catch on fire, spreading rapidly downward until the north wall was a sheet of flames. Volumes of smoke poured in at the open window from the burning wagon, and in a short time through the plastered cracks of the log house puffs of smoke worked outward. Still the doomed man remained doggedly concealed, refusing to reward them by his appearance. The cordon of sharpshooters stood ready to fire upon him the instant he started to run. Fiercer and hotter grew the flames, leaping with mad impetuosity from room to room until every part of the house was ablaze and only the dugout at the west end remained intact.

"Reckon the cuss has shot himself," remarked one of the waiting marksmen. "No fellow could stay in that hole a minute and be alive."

These words were barely spoken when there was a shout. "There he goes!" and a man clad in his stocking feet, bearing a Winchester in his hands and a revolver in his belt, emerged from a volume of black smoke that issued from the rear door of the house and started off across the open space surrounding the cabin into a ravine, fifty yards south of the house, but the poor devil jumped square into the arms of two of the best shots in the outfit, who stood with leveled Winchesters around the bend waiting for his appearance. Champion saw them too late, for he overshot his mark just as a bullet struck his rifle arm, causing the gun to fall from his nerveless grasp. Before he could draw his revolver a second shot struck him in the breast and a third and fourth found their way to his heart.

Nate Champion, the king of cattle thieves, and the bravest man in Johnson county, was dead. Prone upon his back, with his teeth clenched and a look of mingled defiance and determination on his face to the last, the intrepid rustler met his fate without a groan and paid the penalty of his crimes with his life. A card bearing the significant legend, "Cattle thieves, beware!" was pinned to his blood-soaked vest, and there in the dawn, with his red sash tied around him and his half-closed eyes raised toward the blue sky, this brave but misguided man was left to die by the band of regulators who, having succeeded in their object, rapidly withdrew from the scene of the double tragedy.

Champion's pistol and gun were confiscated by some of the gang, and in searching the body a pocket memorandum book was found soaked with his life's blood and bearing a bullet hole through it. Under the printed date of April 9th, the following entry was written in pencil:

Me and Nick was getting breakfast when the attack took place. Two men here with us—Bill Jones and another man. The old man went after water and did not come back. His friend went out to see what was the matter and he did not come back. Nick started out and I told him to look out, that I thought that there was some one at the stable and would not let them come back. Nick is shot, but not dead yet. He is awful sick. I must go and wait on him. It is now about two hours since the first shot. Nick is still alive; they are still shooting and are all around the house. Boys, there is bullets coming in like hail. Them fellows is in such shape I can't get at them. They are shooting from the stable and river and back of the house. Nick is dead, he died about 9 o'clock. I see a smoke down at the stable. I think they have fired it. I don't think they intend to let me get away this time.

It is now about noon. There is someone at the stable yet; they are throwing a rope out at the door and drawing it back. I guess it is to draw me out. I wish that duck would get out further so I could get a shot at him. Boys, I don't know what they have done with them two fellows that staid here last night. Boys, I feel pretty lonesome just now. I wish there was someone here with me so we could watch all sides at once. They may fool around until I get a good shot before they leave. It's about 3 o'clock now. There was a man in a buckboard and one on horseback just passed. They fired on them as they went by. I don't know if they killed them or not. I seen lots of men come out on horses on the other side of the river and take after them. I shot at the men in

42

the stable just now; don't know if I got any or not. I must go and look out again. It don't look as if there is much show of my getting away. I see twelve or fifteen men. One looks like (name is scratched out). I don't know whether it is or not. I hope they did not catch them fellows that run over the bridge towards Smith's. They are shooting at the house now. If I had a pair of glasses I believe I would know some of those men. They are coming back. I've got to look out.

Well, they have just got through shelling the house like hail. I heard them splitting wood. I guess they are going to fire the house tonight. I think I will make a break when night comes, if alive. Shooting again. I think they will fire the house this time. It's not night yet. The house is all fired. Goodbye, boys, if I never see you again.

NATHAN D. CHAMPION.

The above diary written while half a hundred armed men had the house surrounded, with all avenues of escape shut off, with a constant hail of bullets entering from every direction; with his dead friend lying on the floor beside him, knowing, in fact, that these fifty men were thirsting for his blood, is a remarkable production, and will be quoted in history as the utterance of a brave man throughout all time to come. No stronger expression of nerve and heroism has ever been recorded, and coming generations will point to Nate Champion as one of the coolest and bravest men of the Nineteenth century.

The cattle barons branded him a thief, but his neighbors, many of them recognized as fair-minded, honest men, even by the said "barons," declare that he was not a thief, but an honest, hard-working and conscientious citizen; that his life's blood was wanted, not because he would steal cattle, but because his testimony, if given in court, would send two or more of the members of the robber gang to the gallows or to prison for cold-blooded crimes committed. Remembering that these people who thus think and talk have never committed a crime or broken a law of the state, and remembering also that murder, arson, body burning and many attempts to murder are known to lie against the cattlemen engaged in the raid, it seems impossible not to accept the verdict of Champion's neighbors in preference to that of his murderers. The great body of the people have already decided this question and the decision is recorded in Champion's favor.

Nathan D. Champion was born in the country, seven miles from Round Rock, Williamson county, Texas, September 29th, 1857, being the sixth son of Jack Champion and Naomi Standerfer. The family is an old and well connected one, with no scandal attached to its record. By a second marriage of Nate's father there are six sons, making twelve in all, beside six daughters, or a family of eighteen. Nate and his brother Dudley have been in Johnson county for a number of years, coming up with Texas cattle and serving as top hands on many of the big ranches.

Nick Ray was a Missourian, who came to Wyoming as a cowboy and has done faithful work in that line for years. He was black-balled by the stockmen, but his neighbors say unjustly.

CHAPTER VI. THE MARCH TO THE "T. A." RANCH — INCIDENTS BY THE WAY—PREPARING FOR A SIEGE.

After the killing of Champion the

cattlemen joined the supply wagons that had arrived on the creek in sight of the smoking ruins of Nolan's ranch house, and the cooks served a hearty meal to the hungry men. Dr. Penrose, the company's surgeon, and Ed. Towse, the special reporter sent along with the mob by the Cheyenne Sun, reported themselves sick at Tisdale's ranch and deserted. Supper being over, the order to mount was given and a start was made direct for Buffalo, sixty miles away. The ride of thirty miles to the Western Union Beef Company's headquarters was made in five hours, according to several different reports, the object of the forced march being to reach Buffalo before daylight, surprise and capture the town, killing Angus and a long list of others before the people were notified of danger by Jack Flagg. Shonsy, the foreman for the Western Union Beef Company, of which George W. Baxter is general manager, who was with the gang, had about a hundred head of grain-fed horses in the stables ready for the men, and a change was quickly made. With these spirited animals, specially fed for weeks, in anticipation of this emergency, the men dashed off at a rattling pace for what they were pleased to call the "doomed city of the plains." Near Carr's ranch, on Crazy Woman, a camp fire was seen in the road ahead, and the accidental discharge of a gun gave alarm to the invaders, who, supposing it a party of rustlers, on vengeance bent, cut the wire of Carr's pasture fence and made a long detour, reaching the Buffalo road at a safe distance beyond the camp fire.

At 2 o'clock they were at the 28 ranch, twenty-two miles from Buffalo, having ridden thirty-eight miles since leaving the K. C. ruins at sundown, beside losing about an hour's time and covering four or five extra miles. At this ranch coffee was served and two hours' rest taken. At 4 o'clock the march was resumed. When well on the road toward Buffalo a horseman appeared and informed the leaders that there were two hundred excited citizens under arms as a sheriff's posse, in the town, and strongly advised against an attack being made. He said the arrangements made for the assassination of Angus and his deputies the night before had failed by reason of Angus hearing of the killing of Champion and his organization of a posse and departure for Powder river to head off the mob.

This information caused a change of tactics, and orders were given to march to the T. A. ranch and fortify for a strong defense. About this time James Dudley, alias Gus Green, was reported with a broken leg from an accidental discharge of his gun, caused by his horse bucking. He died later on at the military post.

The T. A. ranch was reached shortly after noon and all hands put to work strengthening the position. The following plan was furnished the Daily Leader by a correspondent on the ground during the siege, and is believed to be substantially correct. The buildings are located in a bend of Crazy Woman creek, twelve miles from Buffalo. The house and ice house (marked in the cut) are built of hewed logs, 6 x 8 inches. The stable is also constructed of logs closely fitted together. Log breast works were built on two sides of the house and earthworks inside of the fort. Loop holes were cut, and altogether the position was able to stand off a rifle siege almost indefinitely, did the provisions hold out. In this respect, however, the situation was not encouraging, for the three heavily loaded four-horse wagons of supplies had been captured by the rustlers early in the day, and the sole dependence was the small store at the ranch for the cowboys' use. The supply wagons were found to contain not only provisions, but fuse, giant powder and poison.

Still the "white caps," as the rustlers styled the block house party, were in good spirits, because they had faith in the promises of their "Cheyenne friends" to protect them in the event of an emergency. The emergency had come and their faith was to make them whole.

Terrence Smith had seen and heard

the firing on the K. C. ranch in the morning, and divining its
import, had ridden to Buffalo, notifying the settlers as he went.
Sheriff Angus swore in a posse of 12 men and started about sundown to the relief of his Powder river friends. Meantime other
citizens of Buffalo and countrymen as they came in were being
deputized and armed. Jack Flagg and his stepson rode rapidly
to Grabing, 30 miles, reaching there at 9 o'clock. Securing three
good men as recruits at this point they started back to the assistance of the men they supposed to be still imprisoned at the
K. C. Reaching Carr's ranch at 12 o'clock, they met 12 more
men going on the same mission, having learned the news from
Terrence Smith while on his way to Buffalo. As the combined

47

force was mounting for the start the regulators were discovered approaching, and the little band prepared to ambush them. Fortunately for the murderers, one of the boys let his gun go off accidentally, when the advancing column took the hint and escaped by making a detour as described in a previous chapter.

Flagg's party then went into camp for the rest of the night and in the morning followed on north, passing by the T. A. ranch and reaching Buffalo in the afternoon. Reinforced to 48 men, they rode out to the T. A. ranch and at daylight on the morning of April 11th, the invaders were completely surrounded. Sheriff Angus had in the meantime returned from the K. C. ranch, having ridden 120 miles in the marvelous time of 14 hours, and reported the shooting of Champion and the burning of Ray's body. This news greatly increased the prevailing excitement, and during the day of the 11th a crowd of between three and four hundred well-armed and determined men, making a stand in defense of their homes and their liberty, were on the ground to aid in dislodging the enemy. In the absence of the sheriff, Arapahoe Brown and E. U. Snider were placed in command.

Monday night was devoted to digging rifle pits and throwing up breastworks around the besieged. Tuesday brought recruits from Sheridan county and the distant parts of Johnson, thus swelling the ranks of the home defenders. Early on Monday morning the cattlemen opened fire on a bunch of settlers 400 yards up the hill, and the battle was on. A brisk fire was kept up most of the time from the opening shot until the final surrender. There was not a cannon in the county save at Fort McKinney, and the commanding officer there refused to loan one to the settlers. Realizing that the fortifications were impregnable to small arms and fearing state interference at an early day, it was determined to construct a movable breastwork that could be run down the hill sufficiently near the fort to admit of throwing against its walls the dynamite captured from the cattlemen's supply wagons. For this purpose two of the captured wagons were used. A correspondent on the ground describes this "Go Devil" as follows:

49

The idea of building a movable fort or breastwork originated with Arapahoe Brown and E. U. Snider. The running gear of the captured Arp & Hammond wagons, two pair, were placed side by side several feet apart and then fastened together by a frame work of logs. The rear of the wagons was the front of the fort and was comprised of two thicknesses of eight-inch logs fastened together by wire. This formed a breastwork over six feet high, with five portholes in it, also protected by eight-inch pieces. If necessary baled hay could be placed inside, making the protection still stronger. Five men could slowly move the ingenious contrivance, fifteen could move it easily, and it would protect 40 men. The plan was to move it down upon the white caps near enough to throw giant powder into their fort. It was in working order and had been moved about 100 yards when the soldiers came in sight. All proceedings at once ceased and the men who for 48 hours had held the fighting cattlemen at bay cheered the troops lustily as they advanced to the rescue.

The two days' fight had resulted in no killing on either side, but on Wednesday morning the conditions were anything but promising for the cattlemen. During the previous night rifle pits had been dug within 300 yards of the fort and the Go-Devil, or Ark of Safety, was ready for business. The first bomb sent into the enemies' camp would have forced some of the men from cover and the sharpshooters in the rifle pits would have sent them to earth. Two hours' delay in the arrival of the government troops would have proven, in all probability, fatal to the besieged white caps.

A little after sun-up on the morning of the 13th Colonel J. J. Van Horn filed into camp with three troops of cavalry from Fort McKinney. The colonel, bearing a flag of truce and accompanied by his staff, Captain Parmalee, Governor Barber's aide-de-camp, and Sheriff Angus, advanced to the fort and demanded the surrender of the party. Major Wolcott, in command of the invaders, replied: "I will surrender to you, but to that man, (turning and pointing to Sheriff Angus) never. I have never seen him before, but I have heard enough of him and rather than give up to him we will die right here. He has the best of us now, because our plans have miscarried, but it will be different yet." (The above response of Major Wolcott is as reported by the press correspondent present at the time, and is accepted by the public as true.)

Preparations were at once made for the transfer of the captives to Fort McKinney and in two hours' time they were on the road to the post. The citizens quietly dispersed, many going directly to their homes and others riding into Buffalo. All seemed to be satisfied with the turn of affairs, but all equally insisted that when the excitement cooled off somewhat, the prisoners should be turned over to the civil authorities for trial.

The following is a list of the men who surrendered to Colonel Van Horn:

A. B. Clark, E. W. Whitcomb, A. D. Adamson, C. S. Ford, W. H. Tabor, G. R. Tucker, A. R. Powers, D. E. Booke, B. M. Morrison, W. A. Wilson, M. A. McNally, Bob Barlin, W. S. Davis, S. Sutherland, Alex Lowther, W. J. Clarke, J. A. Garrett, Wm. Armstrong, Buck Garrett, F. H. Labertaux, J. C. Johnson, Alex Hamilton, F. M. Canton, W. C. Irvine, J. N. Tisdale, W. B. Wallace, F. DeBilleir, H. Teschemaker, W. E. Guthrie, F. G. S. Hesse, Phil DuFran, Wm. Little, D. R. Tisdale, J. D. Mynett, M. Shonsey, Joe Elliott, C. A. Campbell, J. Borlings, L. H. Parker, S. S. Tucker, B. Wiley, J. M. Beuford, K. Rickard, Frank Walcott, B. Schultz.

George Dunning, of Idaho, in the confusion incident to the surrender, secreted himself in the loft of the house until dark, when he walked away. He took the "wrong end" of the road and went into Buffalo, where he was arrested by Sheriff Angus and put in jail. R. M. Allen, manager of the Standard Cattle Company, of Ames, Nebraska, had left the party after the K. C. murders, and when met by the news which caused the retreat to the block house, presumably going to hurry up reinforcements, by order of the mob, was captured at Buffalo. Dudley, suffering with a broken leg, had been sent to the military hospital before the T. A. engagement. Another Texan, shot in the groin, was not taken with the party, but sent for later.

A Buffalo paper of April 14th, speaking of the situation just after the surrender, says:

Here in Buffalo all was excitement and unrest; rumors of all descriptions, preposterous, ludicrous and probable, pervaded the atmosphere. No two men could start a conversation but what a crowd would soon gather around. Knots of men could be seen on all street corners, earnestly speculating on the outcome; but for all the utmost decorum and good nature prevailed. But few arrests were made by the officers, and those only for the personal safety of the individual arrested.

Soon after the return of the troops with the prisoners to Fort Mc-Kinney criminal complaints were sworn to before Justice Reimann and warrants for murder and arson issued against these men. Sheriff Angus served the warrants on Colonel Van Horn, demanding the surrender of the criminals to the civil authorities of Johnson county, but his request was denied.

The history of this remarkable siege would not be approximately complete without showing how the rescue was brought about. Hence, the reader will pardon the introduction of copies of the various official telegrams that passed over the wires on the subject.

The private telegraph line from Douglas to Buffalo being in the hands of the cattlemen and no message permitted to pass while the expedition was moving north, was at once ordered opened to business when the gang went into the T. A. fortification. The raiders' friends telegraphed the situation to Acting Governor Barber as soon as the line was repaired, and he immediately opened up communication with Washington, as the public believes, in harmony with previously arranged plans. The delay in repairing the line came nearly proving disastrous to the invaders, for it was late on the afternoon of April 12th when Barber received notice of the perilous condition of his friends. At once the following message was given for transmissal:

(Telegram)
Cheyenne, Wyo., April 12, 1892.

The President, Washington, D. C.:

An insurrection exists in Johnson county, in the state of Wyoming, in the immediate vicinity of Fort McKinney, against the government of said state. The Legislature is not in session and cannot be convened in time to afford any relief whatever or take any action thereon. Open hostilities exist and large bodies of armed men are engaged in battle. A company of militia is located at the city of Buffalo, near the scene of action, but its continued presence in that city is absolutely required for the purpose of protecting life and property therein. The scene of action is 125 miles from the nearest railroad point, from which other portions of the state militia could be sent. No relief can be afforded by state militia, and civil authorities are wholly unable to afford any relief whatever.

United States troops are located at Fort McKinney, which is 13 miles from the scene of action, which is known as T. A. ranch. I apply to you on behalf of the state of Wyoming, to direct the United States troops at Fort McKinney to assist in suppressing the insurrection. The lives of a large number of persons are in imminent danger.

AMOS W. BARBER,
Acting Governor.

To this President Harrison replied as follows:

(Telegram)

Washington, April 12, 1892, 11:05 p. m.
The Governor of Wyoming, Cheyenne, Wyoming:

I have, in compliance with your call for the aid of the United States forces to protect the state of Wyoming against domestic violence, ordered the secretary of war to concentrate a sufficient force at the scene of the disturbance and to co-operate with your authorities. You should have a competent and authorized representative at the place.

BENJAMIN HARRISON.

To this is added the following telegram from General Brooke at Omaha:

(Telegram)

Omaha, Neb., April 12, 1892, 11:37 p. m.
Governor Barber, Cheyenne, Wyoming:

Order of President received and commanding officer at McKinney ordered to prevent violence and preserve peace in co-operation with you. Have you a representative to join the commanding officer? The troops will move at once and will act with prudence and firmness.

JOHN R. BROOKE,
Brigadier General Commanding.

A Washington press dispatch of the 13th says that Senators Warren and Carey were wired from Cheyenne late on the night of the 12th as to the situation at the T. A. ranch, and that they both called upon the president, arousing him from his bed. After consultation the secretary of war was called upon and that distinguished officer was induced to immediately telegraph General Brooke at Omaha, ordering relief from Fort McKinney to the imprisoned cattlemen. As United States Senators, Warren and Carey were the moving power in the case.

Military history fails to record another instance where such prompt action and celerity of movement was had as in this case. Barber's telegram to the president left Cheyenne after dark on April 12. Reaching Washington, 2,000 miles away, a consultation between the president, secretary of war and Wyoming's Senators was held, a telegraph order was flashed to Omaha, 1,500 miles, and in turn transferred to Fort McKinney, another thousand miles, all before 1 o'clock on the morning of April 13th, or inside of six hours. Within another hour three troops of cavalry were in their saddles on the road to the besieged white caps, and before sunrise their bugle notes sounded "rescue" to the waiting barons, 15 miles from the post.

The casual reader of these pages cannot help but note the strange phraseology of Governor Barber's dispatch to President Harrison—"An insurrection exists in Johnson county." There was no insurrection. The people were in arms, but they had taken them in defense of their homes and their lives, against an invading army that was killing citizens, burning homes and laying waste the country as it went. An insurrection is "A rising against civil or political authority; the open and active opposition of a number of persons to the execution of law in a city or state."

Johnson county citizens were doing none of these things unless the invaders were acting under orders of the executive when they marched north to murder and burn.

Another passage in the telegram strikes the informed reader as peculiar—"the continued presence of the military company, (Co. C, N. G.) is required in Buffalo for the purpose of protecting life and property therein." There is no record of Company C having been called out to active duty by the governor until after the sending of the telegram to the president. The truth is believed to be that they were not so ordered out. The captain of the company being a white cap, and fearing lest some of the guns of the company might be pressed into service for use against his friends at the T. A. ranch, ordered and kept a squad of the men at the court house day and night to "watch the guns." The company did no guard duty, as a company, in the

54

town during the siege, and the above executive utterance was entirely superfluous. But it served his purpose, deceived the general government officials and saved his friends.

Wednesday morning, after the surrender, Major Martin received orders from the government to call out Company C and report to the mayor of the town—but the invaders were safe in the hands of Colonel Van Horn before the company members were so called. It is known, also, that the captain of Company C was called on by Sheriff Angus Sunday afternoon, when the first news of the invasion reached the town, and that he refused to obey the sheriff's orders and call out the company to defend the lives and property of his fellow citizens against the approaching enemy. He was ready, however, to act promptly when his friends were in danger.

On the 13th of April Governor Barber telegraphed General Brooke for an escort, to which the following is an answer:

Omaha, Neb., April 13.

Governor Barber:

Your dispatch received. The commanding officer at Fort McKinney reports the surrender to him of Major Wolcott and 45 men, with horses, arms and ammunition, who are being held as prisoners at the post. Under the circumstances I can send a troop of cavalry and transportation for your party to Gillette, or I can send the Wolcott party to Douglas or Gillette, as you may direct. Please advise me of your wishes early.

JOHN R. BROOKE,
Brigadier General Commanding.

The governor changed his mind and replied to the above as follows:

Cheyenne, April 13, 1892, 10 p. m.

General John R. Brooke, Commander Department of the Platte, Omaha, Neb.:

Answering your telegram of this evening, owing to the present excitement existing in Johnson county, it seems best that you should send the Wolcott party with suitable escort to Douglas. I thank you for your kind offer to supply me with transportation and escort from Gillette to Buffalo, but the occasion for this trip at this time is so likely to be entirely dissipated that I will probably not go. Please advise me of your action regarding the Wolcott party.

AMOS W. BARBER,
Acting Governor.

Colonel Van Horn having refused to turn over the prisoners
to the civil authorities of Johnson county, Sheriff Angus sent
the following telegram:

Buffalo, Wyo., April 14, 1892.

Amos W. Barber, Cheyenne, Wyo.:

Make a request on General Brooke to have the commanding officer
at Fort McKinney to surrender the 44 men, now held by him as prisoners, to the civil authorities for trial under the charge of murder.
Warrants have been issued for the above men.

W. G. ANGUS,
Sheriff of Johnson County.

C. H. Parmalee, the white cap sympathizer, learning of Angus'
request, sent the following protest:

Buffalo, Wyo., April 14.

Amos W. Barber, Governor:

The sheriff made a demand this morning upon Colonel Van Horn for
prisoners. He will hold them until his orders are received from the
president. If prisoners should be placed in county jail at Buffalo, I fear
it would not be entirely safe for the peace of the town just at present.

C. H. PARMALEE,
Captain and Aide-de-Camp.

To this the governor replied:

Cheyenne, Wyo., April 15.

W. G. Angus, Sheriff of Johnson County, Buffalo, Wyo.:

Answering your telegram of yesterday, the military authorities will
at the proper time be requested to deliver to the civil authorities the
men now held at Fort McKinney. They will not be delivered until order
and quietude in Johnson county are so fully restored as to convince me
that no further violence will be offered them and that the civil authorities of that county are entirely willing and able to give them the protection which the law requires to be given to all prisoners. An immediate request for their delivery will not be made.

AMOS W. BARBER,
Acting Governor.

Meanwhile, to make doubly sure the retention of the men by
Colonel Van Horn, the following dispatches were forwarded:

Cheyenne, Wyo., April 15.

Colonel Van Horn, Commander, Fort McKinney, Wyo.:

I request that you obtain the custody of and take to Fort McKinney
and there give protection to the men belonging to the invading party

who were arrested before the surrender, and who are now confined in the county jail at Buffalo. This is done in order that all the men belonging to the invading party may be certainly protected from any violence due to the present excitement in that vicinity. I made a similar request upon General Brooke, and have directed Sheriff Angus to deliver the men to you.

AMOS W. BARBER,
Acting Governor.

Cheyenne, Wyo., April 15, 1892.
General John R. Brooke, Commander Department of the Platte, Omaha, Neb.:

I have directed Sheriff Angus to deliver the men belonging to the invading party, who are now in jail, to commanding officer at Fort McKinney.

AMOS W. BARBER,
Acting Governor.

Cheyenne, Wyo., April 15, 1892.
W. G. Angus, Sheriff of Johnson County, Buffalo, Wyo.:

You are hereby requested to deliver at once to Colonel Van Horn, commander at Fort McKinney, the men belonging to the invading party, who were arrested by you before the surrender and are now confined in the county jail at Buffalo. This is done because the excitement and hostile demonstrations in that vicinity require it.

AMOS W. BARBER,
Acting Governor.

Cheyenne, Wyo., April 15, 1892.
Colonel Van Horn, Commander Fort McKinley, Wyo.:

Angus, sheriff of Johnson county, asks that the men who surrendered to you be delivered to the civil authorities of that county. I have declined to make the request for the present for the reason that there seems to be too much danger of the civil authorities not being able to give the men adequate protection against violence.

AMOS W. BARBER,
Acting Governor.

Cheyenne, Wyo., April 15, 1892.
Governor Barber, Cheyenne, Wyo.:

I am assured by the telegraph company that my order of 9 p. m. of the 13th to Colonel Van Horn, reached him last night. Under that order he will hold the Wolcott party until he gets orders from me. The line from Douglas to McKinney ceased working about 2:30 a. m. today.

JOHN R. BROOKE,
Brigadier General Commanding.

57

The fear that the culprits who had deliberately and in cold blood killed two of their fellow citizens might be turned over to the civil authorities where the crime had been committed, so preyed upon the governor's mind that in order to make assurance doubly sure, he wired the secretary of war to instruct the commander at Fort McKinney to deliver the prisoners at Cheyenne, nearly 400 miles distant, and at great expense to the state. To this he received the following reply:

Washington, D. C., April 15, 5 p. m.

A. W. Barber, Governor of Wyoming:

Orders have been sent to General Brooke to deliver to you as soon as he can do so, the captured party under Wolcott.

S. B. ELKINS,
Secretary of War.

These several dispatches show very clearly where the executive heart was, and to the unprejudiced mind explain, in a measure, the lack of official action at an earlier stage of invasion proceedings.

When the news of the burning of

the K. C. ranch reached Buffalo on Sunday, the 10th of April, and
it was learned that the invaders were on their way north with
murderous intent, a feeling of alarm and determination at once
took possession of the people. Robert Foote, the leading mer-
chant of the town, mounted his celebrated black horse and, with
his long white beard flying to the breeze, dashed up and down
the streets calling the citizens to arms. A gentleman present
tells of the picturesqueness of the scene as almost beyond description. Riding up to the front of a store or residence, he would
call out the inmates and in terms as follows address them:

It is the duty of every citizen to protect and uphold the laws of his
country. Wyoming has been invaded. An armed body of assassins has

entered our own county and with bullet and fire have destroyed the lives and property of our people. This same murderous gang is now marching on our village with the open threat to murder our citizens and destroy our property. As men and fellow citizens, who love your homes, your wives and your children, I call upon you to shoulder your arms and come to the front to protect all that you hold dear against this approaching foe. If you have no arms, come to my store and get them free of charge. Our honor, collectively, your honor, individually, and the honor of your common manhood demands immediate action. Fall in line.

The venerable appearance of Mr. Foote, the bold and fearless utterances made in the presence of open and avowed sympathizers of the white caps and friends of the people alike, had the desired effect. In less than on hour a hundred brave men were under arms, ready to lay down their lives in defence of their homes.

They were all sworn in as deputy sheriffs and systematically organized, the city marshal co-operating with them in every detail. Pickets were mounted and stationed well out on all the approaches to the town, and order and discipline everywhere established and maintained. The churches and school houses were opened as quarters for the men, and the good women volunteered their services as in the old Colonial days of our country. As flying couriers carried the news to the country districts the settlers came pouring in, each man with his gun and pistol, and a look of determination on his face that boded no good to the outlaws who dared invade their homes.

Hundreds of men were spared to surround the cattlemen at the T. A. ranch, 12 miles away, but the constant rumor set afloat by the white caps not in the fighting ranks of their friends, that large reinforcements were on the way from the north and the west, kept excitement running high in the town and seemingly made it necessary to keep up an organized force with which to meet any emergency.

Mr. Foote magnanimously and patriotically threw open his store doors to the multitude and supplied every want of the home guards and the besiegers at the T. A. Guns, ammunition, blankets, warm clothing, slickers, flour, bacon, tobacco, canned goods, etc., etc., went out in a constant flow until thousands of dollars' worth had gone to feed and make comfortable the home defenders. The local community, and the state at large, owes a debt of gratitude to this big-hearted and brave old pioneer that it can never suitably repay, yet he will always hold a warm place in the hearts of all honest residents of the state. As the crime of the invasion will never die, so Robert Foote's noble generosity will live always.

To add solemnity and deep seated feeling to the situation during the days of the siege the people realized that the dead and mutilated bodies of two of their fellow citizens were being brought from the ill-fated K. C. ranch for a Christian burial. With this burden of anxiety and trouble upon them the people obeyed the law—maintained order in the town and throughout the county, thereby demonstrating in a most striking manner their loyalty to good citizenship. Sheriff Angus, the most thoroughly abused man in the state, proved himself competent, honest and a man of the people.

Two days after the surrender the burial of Champion and Ray took place, as also that of Coroner Watkins, who had died while engaged in holding an inquest over the remains of the K. C. victims. A newspaper correspondent present made the following mention:

The funeral of Champion and Ray was held at 2 p. m. in a vacant store building on Main street. The room was full of ladies and but few men could get in. The handsome coffins were beautifully and profusely decorated with flowers. Rev. W. J. McCullom, a Baptist, read from the scriptures and then offered prayer, in which he said: "We thank Thee, O God, that there are those who have stood by the law. We pray that the law may be strengthened; that if we cannot get justice here, then in the other world."

Rev. Rader then delivered a few brief remarks. He said: "These men have been sent to eternity. We know not why. They were not criminals. They were of Christian parents. Ray leaves five brothers and three sisters. His parents could not be notified, as the wires were cut. But the same honors have been paid as if they were here."

Many were in tears. Those who had not already viewed the remains were allowed to. A strange sight it was, too. The black and charred trunk of Ray's, with a floral surrounding. The procession then moved up the main street and out to the cemetery. The hearse was preceded by Revs. Rader and McCullom. Then came carriages, wagons, footmen and last, 150 mounted men, three ladies and two boys. There were probably 500 in all. An eight-minute short service was made at the grave by Rev. Rader.

This outpouring of the people to participate in the last sad rites to the departed showed clearly that the masses were arrayed solidly against the law-breakers and assassins, whatever the executive and his coterie of supporters might represent to the president of the United States and his chief advisers. They were not upholders of insurrection, but protestors against the operations of the banditti.

After the funerals the country people generally went home, feeling that they had done their duty and that the backbone of the invasion had been broken, notwithstanding the continued threats of another attempt on the part of the captured cattlemen. They were all ready to "come again," however, should the necessity arise, and did not hesitate to say so in very plain English and in the presence of the non-fighting white caps, who were acting as spies.

No greater proof of the loyalty of Johnson county people, or the "rustlers" of the northern counties, could be given than the following incident:

After Governor Barber had ordered R. M. Allen, who was in the jail at Buffalo, turned over to the military authorities and after receipt of an order from the secretary of war to the same effect, Colonel Van Horn telephoned to Sheriff Angus to know if one troop of cavalry would be sufficient to send over for Allen, or whether he had better send three troops. The sheriff replied: "If you send one or three troops, the chances are that there will be trouble. But if you want your man, detail one soldier."

Accordingly a sergeant was sent in an open wagon, with a driver. When he drove up in front of the court house there were 200 armed men in line on either side of the walk leading from the street to the court house door. The sheriff met the sergeant at the sidewalk, the men fell back, leaving a five-foot open way to the door, through which the sheriff and detail walked, and entering the house, went directly to the jail door.

Allen was brought out, the soldier signed a receipt for him, and the three went to the east door. When Allen saw the multitude of armed men he hesitated and preferred returning to the jail, but the soldier, taking courage from the coolness of the sheriff, ordered and fairly dragged him through the lines to the wagon. No one interfered, or suggested interference, and the city marshal mounting behind the seat occupied by the soldier and the prisoner, they were driven rapidly to Fort McKinney, three miles away.

Knowing that this man had actively participated in the murder of two of their fellow citizens, whose burned and mutilated remains they were then preparing for burial, and believing that his delivery to the military meant his discharge without trial for the crime committed, the spectacle of 200 well armed men standing by and making no protest is a demonstration of the highest type of manhood and a manifestation of supreme respect for the forms of law such as has never before been shown on the frontier, or anywhere else in this broad land. And yet these same men have been called outlaws and a price placed upon their heads by the cattle barons.

Not satisfied with overriding the civil

by the military powers of government in calling upon the president to order Colonel Van Horn and his troops to disband the
sheriff's posse while endeavoring to arrest a mob of men who
had committed murder and arson in the county, Acting Governor Barber again prostituted the civil to the military forces by
seeking governmental power to prevent Sheriff Angus from per-
forming his official duty in the serving of regularly issued warrants for the arrest of these same known criminals. They were
held five days after their surrender within three miles of the
county seat of Johnson county, yet the sheriff, by the strong
military arm of the general government and the order of the
state executive, was not permitted to serve his warrants. Again,
having arrested and lodged in jail some of the participants in

the double murder and arson, the sheriff was ordered by the governor to unlock the iron doors of the prison and turn over the culprits to the military, thus completing a triple prostitution of the civil authorities to military rule.

This is the first time in the history of the United States when, by action of the state executive, the military has been called upon to prevent a peace officer from the discharge of his duty in the execution of the law. It has been reserved for Wyoming's acting governor to bring disgrace and shame upon the state by violating the universal law of commonwealths which demands that he duly enforce the statutes.

Conformably to orders from the War Department and by request of the governor, three troops of cavalry left Fort McKinney on the morning of April 18th in charge of the captured cattlemen, headed for Fort Fetterman. The weather was cold and stormy, but the trip was made without serious mishap. The story had been freely circulated that the "rustlers" would attempt to ambush the prisoners on the road, but this, like many other wild rumors floating among the people, was the work of white cap sympathizers, put in motion to create public sentiment in favor of the returning horde, and thus lessen the hopes of conviction for the crimes committed.

At Fetterman they were met by a detachment of soldiers from Fort D. A. Russell, who took the prisoners in charge and escorted them by rail to Cheyenne, where they were quartered for 60 days at the fort, presumably under military guard. Instead, however, of being confined to their quarters, as other men charged with murder are confined, they were given a very loose rein. The cattlemen spent much of their time in Cheyenne, those having families sleeping at their homes, or in the houses of their friends. The hired Texans had the run of the town at night, very often, and pandemonium reigned in the West end.

Major Wolcott, the commander of the invaders, was released on parole, and made a trip to Omaha and Chicago for the purpose of consulting (the press dispatches said) United States Senator Manderson and other influential persons as to the proper course to take in securing release from the difficulties into which he had led his friends. State Senator John N. Tisdale, another leader of the mob, and others of the gang, were paroled and went to Denver to attend the Masonic Conclave and enjoy themselves. How many others had leave of absence is not known, but it was understood that permits were to be had for the asking.

On the way from the north, and after their arrival in Cheyenne, the mob did not hesitate to publicly declare that they would soon get out of their present trouble, and then they would go back to Johnson county in force and "clean the rascals out." This kind of talk was so common, and certain Republican papers, like the Sun and Tribune, of Cheyenne, echoed and cheered these sentiments to such an extent that the residents of the northern counties lived for months in anticipation of a second raid upon their homes and property.

CHAPTER X. THE KIDNAPPING OF THE TRAPPERS JONES AND WALKER — EYE-WITNESSES OF THE MURDER OF CHAMPION AND RAY.

Believing that Benjamin Jones and

Wm. W. Walker were the only witnesses of the killing of Champion and Ray and the burning of Nolan's K. C. ranch house, prudence dictated the removal of these men from the reach of the prosecuting citizens, and the supreme importance of the work demanded that the conditions of the removal be made liberal and surrounded by no pledges as to the methods to be employed. The injunction was simply: "Get rid of the lying bastards, who would swear our lives away." Accordingly, F. H. Harvey, a lawyer of Douglas, Wyoming, and O. P. Witt, a livery stable keeper of the same place, were employed by the cattlemen, who were backing the invaders, to relieve the country of the presence of these two men at any cost.

Jones and Walker were the two men who had stayed all night at the K. C., April 8th, and who had been captured by the mob on the morning of the 9th, as detailed in a former chapter. After the burning of the house and the shooting of Champion, the two men had been released with the injunction to go south and keep marching, but to hold their tongues as to what they had seen and heard, if they expected to live long and be happy. They came south, reaching Casper after some days. Finding that public sentiment was wholly against the murderers, they told the story of the cowardly attack and brutal murders of April 9th, substantially as related in these pages. This "Trappers' story," finding its way to the ears of the white caps, opened their eyes to the necessity of getting rid of the witnesses and caused the employment of the kidnappers above mentioned.

The details of the spiriting away of these important witnesses has been told by the deputy sheriff of Converse county, who was on the ground and familiar with all the facts. His statement is therefore given here in full and believed to be in strict conformity to the facts. There is ample corroborating testimony, however, so that the case does not rest on Colonel Kimball's evidence, which is as follows:

As is well known, two trappers, Ben Jones and Wm. W. Walker, witnessed the brutal murders of Champion and Ray. After the killing and burning, Wolcott released them and told them to "go south and keep going." They went to Casper. As is well known, Governor Barber refused to deliver the murderers to the proper authorities of Johnson county, but kept them at Fort Russell under military protection, evidently with the intention of turning them loose without trial or punishment. As Sheriff Angus could not arrest them, of course no subpoenaes could be issued for or served on said witnesses, as they could not be cited to appear at any particular time or place to testify. Consequently, said witnesses were free to go when and where they pleased.

Sheriff Campbell was absent at Washington, and Under Sheriff Kimball, the writer hereof, caught on to the fact that the cattlemen were about to attempt to get said witnesses out of the way, even if they had to kill them, and we wrote both Sheriff Angus of Johnson county and Sheriff Rice of Natrona county to be on their guard. The latter began to investigate, and learned that a citizen of Casper had been offered $200 in cash to get Jones and Walker out of town anywhere so that the stockmen could get hold of them. Sheriff Rice informed Jones and Walker of their danger, and they were badly frightened. Casper has no jail or place of safety where they could stay, so Sheriff Rice wired Sheriff Angus of the danger and advised him to take them to Buffalo.

At 2:35 p. m. of May 20th we received the following dispatch:

"Buffalo, Wyo., May 20.

"To E. H. Kimball, Douglas, Wyo.:

"There are two witnesses at Casper in danger of white caps. Have them brought to Douglas and keep safe, and present bill to county. Will write you particulars.

"W. G. ANGUS."

By some means F. H. Harvey knew the contents of that dispatch before we did, and when we took the train for Casper, two hours later, he went along. We went to Casper and saw Sheriff Rice. We went to the witnesses and showed them the dispatch. We told them frankly that they were not prisoners; that we had neither subpoena or warrant for them, and that they did not have to come to Douglas unless they wanted to. They seemed anxious to come. In consultation with Sheriff Rice it was agreed that they should come here, be given arms to defend themselves, and be allowed to sleep in the sheriff's office in the front part of the jail until such time as Sheriff Angus should come or send for them.

The next morning we purchased tickets for them and took them to Douglas in the express car on the regular train. Harvey was also in the passenger coach. At Glenrock, Senator Carey's pet "stock inspector," Higley, took the train and walked into the express car. We cautioned the men to look out for him. He went out, but soon came back and attempted to speak to Jones. Messenger Bennett told him to get out of the car and stay out, and he went. We then became satisfied that Harvey had been employed by the stockmen to either have the witnesses killed or run out of the country, and told them so. Arriving here we gave them rooms in the sheriff's office and each a six-shooter to defend himself. We cautioned them to be careful who they talked to, and under no circumstances to go upon the streets after dark. But Harvey or some of his gang managed to interview Walker during the daytime and got him in a notion of leaving. He told the old man Jones about it, but the latter objected. He wanted to go to Johnson county to testify against the murderers. One night we had to go to Inez and Glenrock on official business. We left a man to sleep in the office with Walker and Jones, not to guard them, but to protect them in case they were attacked. That evening O. P. Witt got Walker, the young man, to take a drink of whisky. That settled it. Walker soon got pretty full, and when night came he refused to go to bed. As he could not be persuaded, Jones said he would walk him back and forth in front of the office and sober him up.

Now, here is Jones' story as told us in Lawyer Fisher's office, in Chadron, in the presence of four other witnesses: He said that they walked about until near midnight. Mr. Walker insisted upon leaving.

He (Jones) objected. Walker said Harvey and Witt had offered them each a horse and saddle and $1,000 if they would leave the country and not testify against the cattlemen, and he was in favor of going. Harvey and Witt came along and took them over to old man Morton's place to talk it over. There they met altogether some eight or ten men, who insisted upon their going. The names of most of them are known and will be given during the coming political campaign. Some of them live here in Douglas. Jones says that they parleyed there for an hour. The gang finally offered them each a horse and saddle and $2,700 cash when they got east of Grand Island, Nebraska. Jones wanted the money then. He told them that he thought that they were just trying to get them out in the country to kill them, and that he would not go with such a gang. He finally told them that there were no charges against him; that he could go when and where he pleased; and that if they would give him a horse and $500 then and there he would leave the country all alone and they had leave to kill him if he ever returned to testify against the Wolcott gang. They refused to do that. One of the gang then told him that he and Walker had got to leave or they would kill them right then and there. Jones said that he would go, provided only one man went along with them, and it was then arranged that Witt should accompany them to Harrison, Neb. Harvey was to take the train and meet them there that evening, and the four would go together to Grand Island, where they were to be paid $2,700 each and given tickets to New Mexico. Jones said it was intended by the gang that it would leave here early in the evening, but it was about 1 o'clock in the morning when three saddled horses were brought out of Morton's stable and he was told to mount a blue roan. Jones said he weakened when he saw the murderous looking gang standing about, and he flatly refused to go, and said he was going to the sheriff's office and go to bed. Instantly guns were drawn and one of the stockmen said: "Get on to that horse, you s— of a b— or I will kill you! We've stood enough of your d—d foolishness." Jones said he thought it meant death anyway, so he mounted the old man Morton's black horse that had been loaned to the gang for the occasion. Walker mounted a red roan and Witt the blue roan, and the three pulled out through a back alley and struck east at a rattling pace.

Jones says they rode upon a keen gallop for perhaps 20 miles, when Witt suddenly stopped and dismounted. He took a lariat from his saddle, threw it over the telegraph wire and pulled it down. He took a pair of wire-cutters from his pocket and cut the wire. Following along to the next post he cut the wire again as high as he could reach. Taking one end of the wire he mounted his horse and dragged the detached piece a long distance and dropped it in the sagebrush. He says that when they left the sheriff's office at dark they each put a revolver in their pocket, but with no intention of stealing them. Witt did not know that they were armed. After riding several miles after cutting the wire

Witt suddenly stopped and said he was lost. Jones said the road was perfectly plain, but Witt insisted that he did not know which way they were going. Witt told them to remain where they were, and he rode off a few rods and commenced lighting matches, one after another. They could see the tops of trees near by. Jones whispered to Walker that Witt was giving a signal and that assassins were probably concealed near there to kill them. Drawing their revolvers, they rode up to Witt and demanded to know what he was doing. He said he was lost and was lighting matches to look at his compass. They knew he had no compass and ordered him to get back into the road. Jones took the lead, Walker following Witt. Jones had the best horse, and he says that from that time until daylight they only hit the high places in the road. They stopped at a ranch to get something to eat, and the lady asked them if they met any strangers going west during the night, stating that about a dozen armed horsemen went past there just before dark. Jones says he is postive that it was the intention of the stockmen to have them murdered there where Witt gave the signal, and that their leaving Douglas late in the night was all that saved them.

When near the Node ranch Witt's horse gave out. He told them to ride on to Harrison. They asked what they should do with the horses. Witt told them to ride into a gulch a mile or so from town, hide the saddles and shoot the horses. After leaving Witt they consulted what best to do. They had but 50 cents between them. Jones wanted to strike across the country. Walker insisted on going to Harrison and taking the train. When near Harrison they hid their saddles and turned their horses loose, but did not shoot them. When they boarded the train at Harrison they were paralyzed with fright to see that Harvey and Witt had a gang of six or seven with them that had got on the train somewhere along the line. They ordered them to take a seat among them in the rear end of the rear car. Jones did not know them, but is sure that they were the gang that intended to kill them the night before. Jones said he expected to be taken from the train and killed at some station, or killed and thrown from the train while it was in motion. It has since been learned that Bill McCann, a miner at Glenrock, Gibson, Wellman, who was since killed in Johnson county, and probably Craig, were among the gang on the train assisting Harvey. Jones says when they arrived at Crawford it was very dark, and before the train fairly stopped McCann and others rushed Walker out of the front end of the car, and Harvey, Witt and one or two others grabbed him and jumped from the rear platform. He did not know where they were, or that they were near a station, and thought they were going to kill him then and there. He drew his gun and told them to stand back or he would shoot. The cowards were afraid to seize him and were trying to reason with him. Marshal Morrison was on hand to arrest Jones and Walker in obedience to a telegram from here. He did not know them, but the gun play and loud talk at the rear end of the train attracted his attention. He demanded to know what the trouble was about. "They are trying to kill me!" yelled Jones. "No, we are not," replied Harvey; "this old man is crazy and we are taking him east to an asylum. I wish you would help us take him over to the B. & M. train." "It's a lie! I'm not crazy!" cried the poor old man; "they are trying to kill me." Just then Witt chirped in: "This man is my uncle and we are taking him to his home in the East. Come, uncle," said he, turning to Jones, "don't act that way; please don't, uncle." "I'm not your uncle!" protested Jones. "Give me that gun," said Morrison. "Who are you?" said the poor old man. "I'm the city marshal here," he replied. "Then, I demand your protection," said Jones; "I am a witness against the men who killed Champion and Ray up in Johnson county and these are cattlemen who are trying to kill me to keep me from testifying against them. They have just killed my partner back there." Instantly the marshal and an assistant put the handcuffs on Jones and Witt and started for the jail. On the way Jones described his partner, whom he supposed had just been killed. The marshal sent Jim Haguewood over to the B. & M. depot, where he nabbed Walker. McCann had just bought two tickets for Grand Island, and he and Walker were about to board the train. Walker was taken up and jailed.

Witt and the two witnesses left Douglas about 1 o'clock Thursday morning. We returned from Glenrock about 1 in the afternoon, and at once set about to discover what had become of them. We had no legal process for holding or detaining them, and we could not have stopped them had they taken the train in broad daylight, but we were afraid they had been killed. We soon learned that Witt had bought and paid cash for two horses the night before, and that he was also missing. We sent a man to interview his partner, Morton, and his answers were so evasive and misleading as to confirm suspicions. We also learned the telegraph wire had been cut near Lost Springs. We then knew well enough that Witt had been paid to run them out of the country, but we had no legal right to stop them. On going to the sheriff's office a little later we discovered that they had taken two revolvers, so we procured warrants and wired Marshal Morrison to arrest them at Crawford, rightly surmising that they would ride east and take the train. That night we got a dispatch from Marshal Morrison that he had them.

The next day we took the train for Crawford, where we arrived a few minutes after a special train had taken Morrison and his prisoners to Chadron on a writ of habeas corpus.

County Judge Ballard, after hearing the habeas corpus case, released the prisoners. Deputy United States Marshal Hepfinger had been brought up from Omaha and, armed with a warrant for the arrest of Jones and Walker on the charge of selling liquor to Indians, the moment the word "released" escaped the lips of the judge he pounced upon the men like a beast of prey, handcuffed them together and rushed them off to a special train, standing at the depot, and in a moment they were moving rapidly for Omaha. Attorney Harvey had secured the warrants from United States Commissioner Darrington on complaint of Witt. Sheriff Dahlman also had warrants for the arrest of the trappers, issued on complaint of Deputy Sheriff Kimball, charging the theft of two pistols, the object being to get the witnesses back into Wyoming and hold them to testify in the cattlemen's cases. Harvey and Witt took the special train for Omaha.

The last chapter in the shameful drama is told in a press dispatch from Omaha, which is here reproduced:

Three bedraggled, unkempt and altogether rough looking men, two of them handcuffed together, and all of them with terror depicted on every feature, huddled in a bunch at the heels of Deputy United States Marshal Hepfinger about 5:30 o'clock last evening as he entered the private office of Marshal Slaughter in the Federal building.

Little attention had been attracted by the party as it moved hurriedly down the long corridor, for the reason that at the hour there were few to notice them. One was Witt, the liveryman, and the two handcuffed together were Jones and Walker. The bracelets were removed as soon as they were safely in the marshal's office and the doors were closed behind them.

Each man carried a heavy, yellow oilskin coat, and none of the prisoners gave evidence of having enjoyed a moment's rest or peace of mind in many a day. They were gaunt and hollow-eyed, and glanced suspiciously at every one and into every corner.

Their arrival disturbed the siesta of United States Judge Dundy, who, although it was long past his usual time of leaving the building had stretched himself on the lounge in Marshal Slaughter's office, as if he had an appointment and fully meant to keep it.

When the prisoners entered the judge slipped across the corridor into his own private office and was closeted with Attorney Frank Ransom, who had likewise been haunting the building for some time, apparently in search of a friend who came not.

Two other attorneys, comparative strangers in town, but who were afterward identified as F. H. Harvey, of Douglas, and H. Donzleman, of Cheyenne, were also flitting about from one office to another and in a very few minutes the entire party, with Prosecuting Attorney Baker, assembled in the office of the District Court and the prisoners were arraigned on the charge of selling liquor to the Indians.

They waived examination and their bond was fixed at $200 each, for which their personal recognizance was accepted. Another adjournment to the office of the marshal followed in order that the men might gather up their belongings, and they then left the building piloted by Attorney Donzleman and Deputy Hepfinger. Marshal Slaughter professed ignorance as to their destination, saying he supposed they were going to supper and that they had also asked where they could get new suits of clothes.

He insisted that he knew nothing about the case, except what he had read in the newspapers, and he did not even know that Deputy Hepfinger was in Chadron until that morning when he received a telegram from him stating that the deputy had arrested his men and would be in that night. They had been arraigned and released on bail, and further than that he was ignorant as a dove.

Deputy Hepfinger could not find time to say a word and Deputy Jackson was but little different. He simply admitted that he was in Crawford Friday and saw the men arrested. He had just sort of happened around to help Hepfinger bring them in, but neither deputy had gone out on that particular business. The marshal "supposed" that Hepfinger had merely been following orders in the way of serving warrants issued by the United States commissioner in whatever part of the state he might happen to be.

The last move in the game was made late tonight (Tuesday).

Attorneys Donzleman and Ransom were busy until 8:30 o'clock filling obscure corners in the rotunda of the Millard, and when a reporter approached the former shortly after that time the bewhiskered lawyer insisted that the whole trouble up in the cattle country had been exaggerated.

But he could not stop to talk. He was going out of the city and would be back in a couple of days, when he would write a book and do several other things. Right now, however, he must catch his train, so good-bye.

He dodged around a little and finally entered a closed carriage waiting at the door. It was not a street hack, but a carriage ordered from the stable for the occasion, and away Mr. Donzleman went.

A few minutes afterward the same carriage dashed around a corner some blocks away and there were four inside and another on the seat with the driver. Inside were Mr. Donzleman and the erstwhile prisoners, Jones, Walker and Witt, and the passenger on the box was the busy Mr. Hepfinger.

They drove straight to the United States marshal's office, which the deputy entered, and after a short wait he resumed his place, and then began the long, rapid drive to West Side station, where the Missouri

Pacific night express was boarded and the fugitives were whirled away to the southward.

It would, perhaps, be unjust to accuse Judge Dundy of knowingly aiding a conspiracy to defeat the ends of justice in kidnaping witnesses from a distant state, but the honest reader cannot escape the conviction that the United States marshal's office was in criminal collusion with the conspirators. The cattlemen's attorney, Donzleman, was in Omaha, in consultation with the marshal. A deputy had been sent to Chadron to serve false papers; that is, warrants issued on a false charge; the attorney and the marshal, having telegraphic information that the witnesses had been arrested and were on a special train, hung about the office awaiting their arrival; the marshal or the attorney, or both, asked Judge Dundy to remain in the office after court hours to hear an important case, and when the prisoners arrived all things were in readiness to at once proceed to business, hear the case and turn the accused loose. Did they have their liberty? Attorney Donzleman and Deputy Marshal Hepfinger took them in charge and the deputy stayed with them until they were placed on the train and sent out of the country. The stop at the marshal's office while on the way to the train further implicates that officer, and the public will always hold him as a party to the damnable job.

When the captured cattlemen got

warmed up in their quarters at Fort Russell and had an opportunity to read the newspapers of this state and from the great
outside world, they discovered that public sentiment was uni-
versally against them, save where the papers had been unduly
influenced, either by money or some other power. Accordingly
the threats of another raid became less violent and the brains of
the baffled "cattle kings" commenced to work on other lines. The
first brilliant thought that seemed to be meaty was martial law
in the northern counties. This would mean the disarmament of
the people of three or four counties and the placing of all the
machinery of the law into the hands of the friends of the cattlemen to be specially run in their interests. It would really mean

75

the barring out of all new settlers and the driving out of many already located, through the oppression always following the enforcement of martial law and the overthrow of the civil authorities.

Impressed with the importance of this idea and still clinging to the belief that the stockmen could control the politics and state policy as of old, the following petition was presented during the summer of 1892:

PETITION FOR MARTIAL LAW

To His Excellency, the Governor, Cheyenne, Wyoming:

Sir—The undersigned respectfully represent that they are the owners of and are interested in, cattle and horses, located and ranging in the county of Johnson, in the state of Wyoming, and in the territory adjacent to said county; that they are citizens of the state of Wyoming and of other states in the Union, and as such are entitled to the equal protection of the law, and to the protection of their property against theft and depredations, and that the county of Johnson and the territory adjacent thereto, is chiefly composed of unclosed lands, especially adapted to grazing, and the livestock of your petitioners and others ranging thereon, is worth several millions of dollars.

And your petitioners further represent that for several years the stealing and misbranding of livestock in the vicinity named has been of frequent occurrence, and has been rapidly growing more prevalent, and that stock thieves continually ride the range and place their brands upon the unbranded calves of other owners and change and alter the brands upon the branded livestock of others, thereby destroying all means of identifying the true ownership thereof. These stock thieves have, during the past year, greatly intimidated and threatened other residents in that vicinity, and have suppressed, by threatened violence, almost all opposition to their unlawful calling and occupation. Their influence, by reason of their numbers, and by their methods of intimidation, has become so great of recent years as to reach the jury box and almost effectually prevent the conviction of any person charged with stock stealing. As one evidence of this the records of the District Court in Johnson county for the five years last past, show that over ————— indictments have been found against different persons charged with the stealing of livestock, and that of this number there have been less than 10 convictions. These acquittals have been so flagrant and so contrary to the evidence that the judges have deplored existing conditions and have declared it almost a useless effort and expense to try any person charged with the stealing of livestock.

These thieves have grown so bold and so open in their support and defense of stealing that they have notified persons who differ with them to leave the country, and have in many instances enforced their threats by acts of violence, and they further threaten to assassinate those who have fled if they return.

In March, 1892, these thieves, together with others whom they had intimidated, met together at Buffalo and organized and arranged for round-ups in violation of law, and were endeavoring to execute the same when certain owners of livestock in that vicinity obtained from the United States Circuit Court for the district of Wyoming an injunction order restraining and enjoining the carrying on of these round-ups. The United States marshal and his deputies who went to the vicinity to serve the order of injunction were grossly mistreated and embarrassed in the service of the process of the court, and found it unsafe to remain there. One of the deputy marshals, George Wellman, a courageous and honest man, was foully assassinated without cause or provocation, on a public highroad in that county while going to Buffalo to receive instructions from the United States marshal relating to the service of his injunction order.

Your petitioners and others intending to enter upon and carry on the round-up arranged for by law, sent trusted and honest employes to attend to the same, and these men were threatened with violence by the thieves and were compelled to leave the county to avoid death or other violence to their persons. During the last two months the number of stock thieves in that vicinity has been greatly augumented by the arrival of other men of the same character from other parts of the country, and there now exists in that country an organized plan of driving the stockmen out, so that their property may become common property for the thieves; cattle are being wantonly and openly slaughtered in that section by thieves, some of the slaughtering being done for no other purpose whatsoever than to gratify malicious motives, and other slaughtering is being done to enable the thieves to market the beef and obtain money therefor. The ranches and homes of owners in that vicinity have many of them been plundered, and the personal effects and furniture there stolen or destroyed, and the occupants of the ranches have been driven from the country by fear. Even women and children at these ranches have received these threats of violence, and have been compelled to seek places of safety. Letters in the United States mails have been opened by these thieves, and there exists a general and well-founded belief that letters and information cannot be safely confided to the United States mails in that vicinity and in several instances persons have been warned against sending letters to their friends upon the outside (of the mail sack), and have been notified not to go to the postoffice either for the purpose of mailing letters or for the purpose of receiving mail therefrom.

No effort of any kind whatever on behalf of the civil authorities in that vicinity is being made to suppress this stealing, or any of the acts of violence and intimidation, and in many instances the civil authorities are, by reason of natural inclination or intimidation, working with the thieves and under their influence. The sheriff of Johnson county openly declares his friendship for those who are known to be thieves, and declares his enmity towards the owners of livestock. With his knowledge, and without any opposition whatever from him, the county is patrolled by large numbers of armed thieves who are permitted to go about heavily armed and prepared at any moment to execute their threat against those who are not in accord with them.

In conclusion, your petitioners represent unto your excellency that there exists in the district named an armed combination to prevent the administration of law and justice; that neither life nor property is in any respect safe, and does not and cannot receive protection at the hands of the civil authorities. The country named is in a feverish state of excitement and under a complete reign of terror, and both persons and property are wholly at the mercy of the outlaws and thieves who infest that section.

We, therefore, pray your excellency will place the district named under martial law, for the reason that it is the one remedy for the existing evils, and it is the only way of protecting the lives and property of the people there.

Respectfully submitted,

(Signed)

Trustees of Pratt & Ferris Cattle Company, by J. A. Pratt, Manager.
Clay & Forest.
Henry A. Blair.
Wm. A. Paxton.
Windsor, Kemp & Co.
E. S. Rouse Boughton.
John N. Tisdale.
Fred G. Hesse.
A. R. Powers.
Henry G. Hay.
Manhattan Cattle Company, by H. G. Hay, President.
Ogallala Land & Cattle Company, by W. C. Irvine, Manager.
Clark & Hunton.
A. B. Clarke & Co.
Conrad & Clark.
Murphy Cattle Company.
E. W. Whitcomb.
The Western Union Beef Company, by Geo. W. Baxter, Manager.
Jas. G. Pratt.
Bay State Livestock Company, by H. H. Robinson, Superintendent.

To the reader of these pages who has kept the run of events as they have been detailed, the above can only be viewed in the light of a tissue of false statements from beginning to end, and as a last dying effort to accomplish by strategy what the signers of this petition, or their agents, had failed to do in an open fight on the grassy plains of Northern Wyoming.

Up to the time of the filing of this libelous petition no act of violence had been perpetrated in Johnson county, or any other northern county, save by the cattlemen themselves, or their hired assassins. The threats, intimidation and murder were all on the side of the cattlemen. True, George Wellman had been killed, but the well-settled conviction then, and now, rested and rests in the minds of the public that this unfortunate young man was the victim, not of the settlers of Johnson county, but of the cattlemen themselves. That the murder of George Wellman was planned in Cheyenne and the brutal outrage executed on orders from the Capital City seems of easy demonstration to all fair-minded men.

What are the facts? For years the stockmen had dominated the north—its hills, valleys and plains were overrun with their lowing herds. As time wore on the hardy pioneer came to dispute with them the occupancy of the rich lands and to build homes where before were seen only the dashing cowboy and the long-horned steer. This was an innovation not to be tolerated. A few cattle were stolen—as is the case in all communities—but no act of violence was committed. Exasperated at the situation and realizing that no serious charges could be successfully preferred against the settlers—the series of cold-blooded murders heretofore mentioned in these pages was perpetrated at the hands of the cattle barons. Still no overt act was done by the settlers. Then the raid was undertaken for the purpose of terrorizing the country. This failed of its purpose, though 48 men crimsoned their hands with the blood of their fellow citizens. Still no blood stains were upon the hands of the settler. They rose up in their honor and their might to defend their homes and their lives against the swoop of the assassins, but they committed no crime.

Baffled at every turn, what more natural to a band of men who had done murder, arson and body burning, than to order the death of one of their trusted aiders if, by so doing, they believed that they could fasten the crime of assassination upon the innocent settler and use the circumstance as a lever to force the declaration of martial law in the country they were trying to conquer? With Wellman dead, and the crime of his murder laid upon the settler, it was believed that the governor could be induced to place Northern Wyoming virtually in the control of the then defeated cattlemen, through the agency of the marshals who would supercede the civil authorities in the event of martial law being proclaimed. With martial law in force in Johnson, Converse, Natrona and Weston counties, as was contemplated by the above recorded petitioners, the defeat at TA ranch would be turned into a great victory. To accomplish this by the loss of one of their friends would be, from their standpoint, gaining much for a little. They would not stop to consider the matter in the light of the infamy that should attach to an act of such base treachery, for would it not save many of their own lives by accomplishing what it would require another raid into the county to as successfully do? And with the aroused feeling everywhere prevalent was it not almost a certainty that some one of the faithful would be called upon to pay the final debt of nature? The chain of circumstances is very damaging to the professed innocence of the cattlemen's ring.

Exactly what impression this document had upon the mind of the acting governor will probably never be known to the public. Neither will it be known just what action he took in the premises, unless a thorough and far-reaching investigation is made by the Legislature. But the suspicion is strong in the minds of most well-informed persons that the subject matter was laid before our United States senators and the president, with a request that action be taken by the general government. This impression prevails by reason of the subsequent action of the secretary of war in quartering soldiers for months in two of the northern counties, a thing unknown before in the history of the country during a time of peace, and the issuing of a proclamation by President Harrison calling upon the citizens of Wyoming to lay down their arms and repair to their homes, or by implication, that martial law would be declared within three days of that official notice. This being done at a time when the invaders were in the hands of the military at Fort Russell, and when no armed body of men was to be found anywhere in the state, save the soldiers at the two government posts, makes it difficult of explanation except on the theory that a copy of the above quoted petition, setting up a false condition, had been presented to the president, and his interposition specially urged, either by the governor or the United States senators at that time representing the state in Congress.

It is understood that the main object of Major Wolcott's parole trip was to secure senatorial influence in urging the president to declare martial law, and perhaps Senator Manderson and some others joined the Wyoming senators in this outrageous demand.

The first fruits of the cry for martial law are made manifest in the following telegram:

Washington, June 6, 1892.

Six troops of cavalry from Fort Robinson, Nebraska, are ordered to march to Powder River, Wyoming. The two troops of cavalry at Fort McKinney are directed to join them. Six troops of cavalry from Fort Niobrara, Nebraska, are ordered to march into Wyoming, going into camp at a point between old Fort Fetterman and old Fort Casper.

These cavalry forces moved as directed, and remained stationed in the sagebrush all summer, apparently as a forerunner of martial law. Common rumor had it that the regulators believed the presence of the troops would so incense the settlers that some overt acts would be committed and such serious trouble follow as to make martial law necessary, or at least excusable. The northern press "caught on" to this idea, and strongly urged upon the people to bear patiently this humiliation and give no cause for further action by the government. Such advice was hardly necessary, but there was no disturbance at the camp on the Platte river.

At the Powder river camp there was trouble, but it was so

plainly the result of viciousness on the part of the soldiers that no action looking toward martial law could be taken by the authorities. Two of the colored troops get into a row with a depraved white man over a lewd woman at a bagnio in the village of Suggs, a mile from the camp. The night following, between 10 and 11 o'clock, a squad of 44 colored troops marched into the town and opened fire on a saloon where a number of men were assembled, playing cards and drinking. The attack was unprovoked and unexpected. The citizens, however, rushed for their guns and pistols, and charged the black soldiers, driving them out of town, killing one and wounding five. It was claimed that some of the friends of the white caps were in the soldiers' camp at the time, and the responsibility was charged to them. No further trouble occurred.

As confirmatory of the impressions that the sending of troops into the state was the result of the misrepresentations of the interested stockmen, and that they hoped it would turn out to be a move in their favor, the following statement of an officer stationed at Omaha, and made to an agent of the Associated Press reporter on June 11th, 1892, may be quoted, as follows:

It is believed by the military authorities that the presence of a large body of troops in the cattle districts will have a quieting effect, and in case it becomes necessary to take active steps to quell another outbreak, the troops will be close to the scene of the disturbance. The department is convinced that there are a number of thieves of that region who are agitating this bitterness and are at the head of this lawlessness that has terrorized portions of the state. These thieves will be watched very closely, and about the first break they make they will be taken in by the powerful arm of Uncle Sam.

One of the officers at the headquarters was asked today if he thought the state of Wyoming would be placed under martial law and he replied that he did not think it would be necessary to adopt that measure. "There is one thing you may depend upon, however," he said, "the government is not going to put up with the lawlessness out there any longer. That business has got to come to an end, and my opinion is that if you watch matters closely you will see an emigration from Wyoming of some of the parties who have been busy stirring up the trouble."

The last remark quoted above has proven true—some of the stockmen who were "busy stirring up the trouble" have "emigrated," and others are likely to follow suit, but the settlers who took up arms to defend their homes remain, and no hired assassins can drive them out.

The soldier quartering scheme failing to produce the desired effect, some occult influence was brought to bear on President Harrison, and he issued the following:

PROCLAMATION

Whereas, By reasons of unlawful obstructions and assemblages of persons it has become impracticable, in my judgment, to enforce by the ordinary course of judicial proceedings the laws of the United States within the state and district of Wyoming, the United States marshal, after repeated efforts, being unable by his ordinary deputies, or by any civil posse which he is able to obtain, to execute the process of the United States courts;

Now, therefore, be it known that I, Benjamin Harrison, president of the United States, do hereby command all persons engaged in such resistance to the laws and the process of the courts of the United States, to cease such opposition and resistance and to disperse and retire peaceably to their respective abodes on or before Wednesday, the 3rd day of August next.

In witness whereof, I have hereunto set my hand and caused the seal of the United States to be affixed. Done at the City of Washington this 30th day of July, in the year of our Lord one thousand eight hundred and ninety-two, and of the independence of the United States the one hundred and seventeenth.

(Seal)   BENJAMIN HARRISON.
By the President:
JOHN W. FOSTER, Secretary of State.

No more infamous document ever issued from official pen. No greater outrage was ever perpetrated upon a long-suffering people than is here ruthlessly thrust upon all of Wyoming's citizens. The statements made in the "whereas" were absolutely false in every line. They were lies, pure and simple. On the day that the text of this insult reached Cheyenne a prominent citizen approached Judge Riner, of the United States Court, and asked him what the proclamation meant. His reply was that he knew absolutely nothing about it. That he was as much surprised as any other citizen—that there were no processes issued from his court, but what had been served in the regular way— no obstructions having been met with by the marshals that had come to his knowledge. Every person then living in the state knew that there was no resistance to law within our borders, and that there was no body of men collected anywhere to whom an order to "disperse and retire peaceably to their respective abodes" could possibly be addressed.

How came it, then, that the president of this great country should descend to the level of a blackmailer, and by an official act proclaim to the world that the good people of an entire state were engaged in resisting the law?

There is but one explanation—the statements in the petition to Acting Governor Barber had been presented to him as the truth, and he had been deceived by senatorial representatives into believing them. It was the influence of the old Cheyenne cattlemen's ring permeating official ranks from the policeman on his beat up through all the gradations to the White House at Washington. It is said that our senators denied any knowledge of this proclamation until it appeared. This may be true, but the public is slow to accept it as a truth. How did the president gain the information upon which to base his statements? Certainly, he would not accept such grave charges as true without an investigation. Should he investigate, where would he begin? Manifestly with the senators from the state implicated. Were the statements filed by the governor, no sane man, sitting in the presidential chair, would act on them without consultation, when there were two senators to whom he could apply for confirmation or denial of the charges. There is no escape from a division of the responsibility of the president's defamatory proclamation between the acting governor and the two senators representing Wyoming at that time, and the public will so hold.

A few weeks after the arrival of

the invaders at Fort Russell it was determined by them and their friends to regulate, or muzzle the press of the state. It had been claimed that all of "the best citizens" approved the raid with its red-handed murders. There were some newspapers, however, that dissented from this view, and that did not hesitate to call murder and arson by their proper names. To be held up to public gaze as guilty of cold-blooded murder did not suit the sensitive natures of the men who had merely killed two of their fellow citizens in one day and burned the body of one of them while they sat around the camp-fire meal and joked about the incense that rose from the burning pile. This sort of talk must be stopped.

Colonel E. H. Kimball was editing a paper at Douglas, Wyoming, and he dipped his pen in gall each week when speaking of the outrages committed by this gang of outlaws. He printed their names in full and told just what crimes they had committed. He must be destroyed and the power of his press overcome. So a dozen or more of them filed informations against him for criminal libel. One of the charges was made by George W. Baxter, of Cheyenne, General Manager for the Western Union Beef Company. Upon this a warrant was issued and Colonel Kimball was kidnaped and brought to Cheyenne, where he was lodged in jail. He was held for 30 days before he could give bonds, the law requiring bondsmen to be residents of the county where the accused is in prison. This had the effect of temporarily stopping the issue of the paper as Colonel Kimball was a poor man and could not hire the work done while he remained in jail. The case never came to trial.

The editor of the Northwestern Livestock Journal offered to sign the bonds of Colonel Kimball, and as a reward his paper was boycotted by the cattlemen in anyway connected with the raid. Later four of them entered his office one day and made a personal attack upon him, undoubtedly with murder in their hearts. But their designs were frustrated and the editor still lives.

The next attempt to regulate the tone of the press was made by this same man Baxter on the Cheyenne Daily Leader, because it dared to condemn the work of the assassins. He owned a few shares of the Leader stock and began an action for the appointment of a receiver so as to get control of the columns and shut off the truth about the invasion and its supporters. The trial was long and expensive, but finally resulted in a withdrawal of the complaint. These efforts at destroying the press were so barren of success that it was concluded to make no further attempts in that direction.

CHAPTER XIII. GOVERNOR BARBER PERMITS JOHNSON COUNTY OFFICERS TO SERVE WARRANTS ON THE INVADERS — PECULIAR CONDITIONS PRECEDENT — CHANGE OF VENUE GRANTED BY JUDGE BLAKE.

J. W. Blake, judge of the Second Ju-

dicial district, which comprises Johnson and Albany counties, sent a letter to Acting Governor Barber on the 19th of June, requesting that he deliver to the authorities of Johnson county the stockmen then confined at Fort Russell. The judge informs the governor that he has received a certified copy of informations filed against 44 persons, charging them with murder.

I have also received a certified copy of warrants issued by the clerk of the court for the arrest of the parties charged in the information.

The men against whom the informations are found are confined at Fort Russell under absolute control of the War Department. The courts, before they can exercise their functions, must have the control of the persons whom they accuse of offense of the law.

87

In view of these conditions I make the following requests:

First—That you turn over to the sheriff of Johnson county or his deputy, the parties named in his warrants, and give them into his custody at Fort Russell.

Second—That before you do this you inform me of the time you will be ready to make the transfer in order that I may give the officer full directions as to the place they shall be held, pending the future proceedings of the court. Pending the time of the trial, I believe it my duty to exercise the utmost diligence and care—first, in placing the prisoners within the custody of the proper officers of the court; second, that they be kept with absolute safety; third, that these things be done in such a way that will entail the smallest possible expense upon Johnson county.

I do not consider it necessary at this time to have these men taken to Johnson county. I have in view two methods of holding them in custody, both of which will require the assent of the parties accused.

One is that they be confined at Fort Russell as long as the War Department will detain them there; the other that they be confined in the north wing of the penitentiary at Laramie, a portion of the building now unoccupied for any purpose, and where they will not under any circumstances come in contact with any of the convicts confined in another part of the building.

Should you surrender these men to the judicial department upon this request, my positive order will be given to the officer to whom they are surrendered upon these points in the way I have indicated as to their confinement, and I am satisfied beyond any question that these orders will be obeyed, for the reason I believe that I have a right to make them, and I have never known an officer of Johnson county to disregard any direction I had given him. I must urge upon you, that I insist as soon as the matter can be arranged, wherever these prisoners are detained, they must be kept under the custody of an officer of the court for Johnson county.

Up to this time the acting governor had refused to permit the Johnson county officers to serve the warrants on the confined cattlemen, notwithstanding almost daily applications had been made for that privilege. After the receipt of the above communication the matter was given careful executive consideration, and on the morning of July 5th, 1892, Governor Barber escorted the prisoners to Laramie City, where Judge Blake was sitting "in chambers." Adjutant General Frank Stitzer, accompanied by almost the entire military staff of the governor, marched the cattlemen to Hesse's hall, a large room previously engaged as headquarters for them. Here they were formally turned over to Deputy Sheriff Roles, of Johnson county, who took charge of them. They were made comfortable in their new quarters and seemed to have little care about the future turns their case might take.

An application for a change of venue from Johnson county was made, heard and granted, but two weeks' time was consumed in the selection of a place, Cheyenne finally being chosen. The attorneys for the prosecution objected very strongly to having the trial carried to Cheyenne on the grounds that that city was the head center of the old dominating cattle influence, and the feeling of sympathy worked up in favor of the accused, many of whom had been prominent in political, business and social circles, would prevent an unbiased hearing of the case. This idea was fought by the lawyers for the defense, and many witnesses were called on either side. When Cheyenne was decided upon the opinion in many parts of the state was freely expressed that the cattlemen had won, and that the trial would be a howling farce. It was honestly believed by many people that the tentacles of the old gang were so securely fastened in the people of that city that they could control the findings of juries as they had in the past shaped the legislation of the state. From that time forward interest in the case lessened among the masses and they began to agitate the question of how to counteract this un-American system of intrigue and conspiracy that was so rapidly undermining our republican form of government.

The prisoners were returned to Cheyenne, put in charge of Sheriff A. D. Kelly, and ostensibly quartered in Keefe's hall, instead of the jail. The first night after their arrival the cattlemen proper of the gang were given a champagne banquet at the clubhouse by their white cap friends, and it was a night of high revelry. During the entire term of their waiting for the sitting of the court the cattlemen slept at their homes or the hotels, and the entire party took their meals where they chose, and had the run of the town day and night. A full list of guards was employed at the expense of Johnson county, and the prisoners were supposed to be kept in their quarters continually, save when they were escorted to their meals. The truth of the situation is well and fittingly illustrated by the following incident:

A newspaper man wanted to interview some of the confined men one evening about 8 o'clock. He found three guards on duty at the front door, and asked to be shown in to see the prisoners. He was escorted inside but found no one present. Being somewhat surprised, he asked how this happened. The reply was, "The guards are on duty, sur, and if yez wants to foind the prisners, yez must go where they are; oill not foind 'em for yez."

Another incident may be mentioned as giving a sort of object lesson. One morning soon after the return of the regulators to Cheyenne the writer hereof was going down the street to his office, when he observed one of the imprisoned men come to the door in his night shirt, reach out through a partial opening and get the morning paper lying on the door sill. A block farther down he saw another invader taking his morning walk. Two blocks farther a city policeman was met, driving in front of him four tramps, each with a chain fastened to his leg and a 50-pound weight on his shoulder, being marched to work on the streets.

The contrast was striking—the cattlemen, crimsoned with the blood of their fellowmen, given the freedom of the town and indulging in riotous living—the tramps, with no crime charged against them but that of asking for bread, placed in the chain-gang and driven like beasts to break stones on the highway. Comments would only weaken the case—the reader must draw his own conclusions.

On August 7, 1892, the invaders were

arraigned before Judge Scott, in the District Court for Laramie county, at the courthouse at Cheyenne. They all pleaded not guilty, and the work of securing a jury began. Three days were consumed and some progress made. It was evident that a jury could be found in the county, and hopes began to be entertained that the prisoners would be called upon to face their accusers for the killing of Nathan D. Champion and Nick Ray, and the burning of the Nolan ranch on Powder river, April 9th, 1892. Skeptics and doubters there had been from the time of the arrest of the prisoners. "They never will be tried," was an expression heard every day, and in all parts of the state. The theory was that the cattlemen exerted such a dominating influence that in some way they would prevent a final hearing and that the accused would go free. The special privileges granted the prisoners throughout the summer months strengthened this idea, but when the day of trial came and both prisoners and witnesses appeared in court, the doubters began to hope that they were mistaken in their judgment.

But a bomb shell was already loaded, with fuse attached. At the close of the third day the sheriff, A. D. Kelly, presented a petition to Judge Scott for relief, setting forth that Johnson county was bankrupt; that its officials had not paid the expenses incurred by the detention of the prisoners in Albany county pending the hearing on the motion for a change of venue; that the cost of holding the prisoners, including hall rent, guards and food, was over a hundred dollars a day; that he could not get any money from the county officials with which to meet these bills; that Johnson county warrants would not take the place of money; that he, as sheriff, would no longer assume responsibility for these current expenses, and praying for an order of court that would secure him against loss as he could no longer hold the accused.

When court convened on the morning of August 10th Judge Scott handed down his decision on the above named petition in substance as follows:

I am unable to issue an order compelling Johnson county to make good the sheriff's disbursements for the maintenance of the prisoners, and as he has refused to longer provide for them, my only alternative is to admit them to bail. But as the defense refuse to furnish bail, I am forced to release them on their individual recognizances.

The prisoners at once signed each his own bail bond for $20,000 in the two separate cases, and they were all set at liberty, but ordered to appear at the next term of court, in January, 1893.

When this news reached the public a feeling of disgust was everywhere manifest, save among the white caps, who flung their banners on the outer walls and literally colored the town crimson. It was then clearly demonstrated that the old guard had gotten in its work, and that crime was still to go unwhipped of justice. The press of the country was generally outspoken in denunciation of the travesty upon justice, and many very bitter editorials were printed. The following from the Cheyenne Daily Leader is a sample of the more conservative utterances:

THE PRISONERS RELEASED

Well, the stockmen and Texans are all at large, having been released yesterday on their own recognizances. Taking it all around perhaps it's just as well. Their confinement at Keefe hall was such only in name. They were permitted to go at will day or night about the city. Many of them never slept in the hall at all, and the guards were an elegant superfluity except whenever it was necessary to preserve the peace among the Texans. Some of the prisoners took in the Templar demonstration at Denver, and few of them were ever impeded in any of their movements.

The keep of the prisoners, pay of guards and hall hire, amounted to about $100 a day. For all practical purposes this amount of money was but little better than wasted. In the ordinary sense of the term the prisoners were never guarded and could have made good their escape at any time were they so minded. Such scenes as were presented could not, in the nature of things, increase the public respect for the law or its administration, and from this point of view it was better to discharge the prisoners even on their own recognizances than to pretend to keep them in custody when they were as a matter of fact freer to go about than men employed at the shops.

Thoughtful persons asked why Governor Barber had brought these men hundreds of miles from the scene of their misdeeds to be held at the expense of Johnson county, and ready money demanded at every turn in the case? Johnson county's credit was good at home and abroad—her warrants had always been paid and her people would have been glad to furnish guards and provision for the invaders and taken their pay in evidences of indebtedness, knowing that they were good for their face value. This privilege was denied them, and the costs more than doubled by transferring the case to distant points for a hearing. Beside this the white cap press continually held Johnson county up as a bankrupt community and insisted that it could never pay the cost of a trial. This tended to weaken or destroy her credit away from home and rendered the borrowing of money difficult. Looking at the train of circumstances as a whole, and connecting them with the final release of the prisoners without trial, on the plea of Johnson county bankruptcy, the consensus of opinion in many circles was that the 10th of August witnessed the closing act of a drama (if such a comparison may be allowed) fully outlined before the prisoners left Fort McKinney for Cheyenne under military escort. The fact that confidence in their ultimate release never seemed to be lacking in the minds of the invaders strengthens this view of the case. They apparently knew what was to be the outcome.

There were many ludicrous and humiliating incidents connected with the detention and partial trial of these men. They were under arrest for murder, in the hands of the law and the sheriff, yet when arraigned in court to plead F. M. Canton was carried in on a stretcher, wounded by the accidental discharge of his own pistol while in one of the city saloons in the early morning hours. This was made the excuse for asking an order of court to disarm the prisoners, and as there was a living example of the danger before the court, the order was granted. This was the 7th day of August, and the prisoners had been in custody since April 13th—all this time carrying the arms and flaunting them in the face of the law, while the citizens walked the streets with no weapons of defense.

Another incident is worthy of relating. A brother of Nathan Champion came in on the afternoon train from the west. Desiring to see the men who had killed his brother, he asked the first man he met on the street where they were to be found. He was directed to Keefe hall. Approaching the entrance he found no one on guard at the door, so he went inside and slowly walked around the room, deliberately looking at the men as they sat or lounged about. For a wonder, there happened to be about half the prisoners in the hall at the time, and two or three of the cattlemen who were personally acquainted with the murdered Champion. When they saw this man approaching they thought it was the ghost of the murdered man, and rushed for an officer to put him out. The deputy sheriff asked: "Who are you, and what do you want here?" He replied: "My name is Champion, and I came in to see these men who killed my brother Nate." The deputy quietly walked by Champion's side and told him he had better retire as visitors were not allowed without a permit. "All right," said Champion. "I have seen the murderers, and have no further business here," walking out, as he finished this remark.

The presence in the city of a brother of Nate Champion seemed to stir up unpleasant memories and create forebodings in the minds of the imprisoned cattlemen for apparently well authenticated rumor said that an express wagon was driven up to the rear of Keefe hall just at dusk the evening after the above named visit, and 40 Spencer rifles unloaded for the use of the prisoners in the event of an attack by "rustlers or their friends." No attack was made or contemplated, but all the same there was a good deal of nervousness displayed for several days, and Champion's ghost seemed to have taken possession of Keefe hall, much to the disgust of the temporary sojourners therein.

Immediately on the signing of their bonds, preparations commenced for leaving the city. The Texans and many of the cattlemen took the afternoon train for the East. The fiscal agents of the Stock Association were part of the outgoing throng, which laid over a day in Omaha to settle up with the hired men. These were supposed to be on the pay-roll at $5 a day from the time of their enrollment in March up to the hour of their discharge by the court, as well as for the computed time of their journey home. The Omaha papers of the 12th and 13th of April announced the happy adjustment of these financial arrangements and the departure of the late imprisoned on their way south in the best of spirits and with canteens well filled.

Tom Smith, the captain of the Texans, has since paid the last penalty. He was shot and killed by a negro desperado on the cars between Gainesville, Texas, and Guthrie, Oklahoma, in the summer of 1893. Others of the band are reported killed, but how many is not known. He who lives by the sword shall perish by the sword, will no doubt prove true with many of these reckless characters.

A goodly number of the cattlemen quietly departed for a change of air, while others repaired to their respective places of domicile. One general manager, who had been in the north for years, remarked that he was "heading straight for Brooklyn, and that once safely over the bridge he would stay on that side of the East river. He had had all the business he wanted with a lot of duffers who had no more sense than to shoulder their guns and fight like demons for their jim crow farms in a country that was not worth a d—n only for cattle grazing." He has kept his word.

January 21st, 1893, when the case of the State of Wyoming vs. the Invaders was called nearly all of the cattlemen responded, but the hired men failed to appear. Alvin Bennett, prosecuting attorney for Johnson county, offered a motion to enter a nolle prosque, to which the attorneys for the defense entered an objection. After discussion the court accepted the motion and the prisoners were discharged. A similar motion was made covering the cases of the hired Texans, who had not appeared, and an order of discharge was entered in the court records, also one rescinding the order of forfeiture of bail bonds previously entered.

This action was severely criticized by many as unwarranted and outrageous, but the public finally settled down to the common opinion that the ring had so many obstructions of one kind and another to spring that justice was not likely to be meted out in the event of a long and expensive suit, and perhaps it was as well to end the farce without further cost to Johnson county settlers. It presented one object lesson that would in the end result in good to the state by arousing a sentiment among the masses in opposition to corporation rule that in future would prevent similar disgraces.

April 4, 1893, the Wyoming Stock-

growers' Association met in annual session at the court house in the city of Cheyenne. John Clay, Jr., of Chicago, president of the association, was in the chair, and according to the report of the committee on credentials, there were present 99 members in good standing.

Mr. Clay delivered quite a lengthy address immediately after calling the meeting to order, and after alluding to the general situation of the cattle industry and talking about bad markets, etc., etc., he said:

Not content with the imposition of financial and climatic troubles another burden had to be added to our lot. After a long period of forebearance and patience from range depredations, both petty and wholesale, the trouble culminated a year ago and the so-called invasion of Johnson county took place, which ended unfortunately and gave rise to an almost interminable amount of bad blood, politically and socially.

97

After moralizing for some time on the low state of Wyoming public sentiment that he admitted was with the Johnson county settlers and against invaders, he continued as follows:

While the invasion is now consigned to history, it developed during its progress last spring and the long, weary summer months which followed a spirit of admiration from all classes of the men (the very flower of Wyoming's citizens) who had taken part in the expedition. Under the most trying circumstances they stood shoulder to shoulder, scarce a murmur escaping them. Gentlemen, I am not here to defend these parties. Technically, legally, they did wrong, but I consider it no mean privilege to stand in this prominent position today and say that I count everyone of them a friend. Notwithstanding their errors of judgment, we respect them for their manliness, for their supreme courage under the adverse fire of calumny and the usual kicking a man gets when he is down. There will be a day of retribution, and the traitors in the camp and in the field will be winnowed like wheat from the chaff.

Later in the day, when "the good of the order" was sprung for general discussion, Henry G. Hay, treasurer of the association, closed a speech of general approval of the stockmen's methods of cattle seizure by the inspectors of the Livestock Commission, intimidation, etc., with the following sentence: "I love the association for the enemies it has made, as they are nearly all thieves and rustlers."

These utterances of the officials of the stock association in an open, public meeting, and the hearty endorsement they received from the ninety and nine members present, very clearly prove that the public was right when it declared at the time of the invasion, the responsibility of that outrage rested upon the Wyoming Stockgrowers' Association. The invaders and the stock association are now quite generally used as synonymous terms among the people.

An analysis of these "official utterances" is unnecessary, because each reader will do that for himself, but it is well, perhaps, to call attention to the threat made in the closing sentence of John Clay, Jr.'s speech: "There will be a day of retribution." Is this a warning that there will be another invasion? Another band of hired assassins brought into the state to murder and burn, and in such numbers as to overcome all resistance? Is another and greater attempt to be made to overthrow the state constitution, drive the settlers from their homes and reinstate the cowboy as the ruler of the country? That is the plain English of the "official threat." But he was probably talking through his hat.

It might be pertinent to here inject this inquiry: "Can an organization whose officers openly countenance murder, arson and body-burning, and denounce all who differ from them in opinion as thieves and rustlers, be looked upon by a community as an upholder of the majesty of the law and a friend of society?"

CHAPTER XVI. SOME MATTERS INCIDENTAL TO AND CONNECTED WITH THE INVASION.

It was claimed in the invaders' petition

to the governor and in his dispatch to the president, and talked in the press as well as on the street that the civil authorities of Johnson county refused to give protection to the cattlemen while engaged in their legitimate business of gathering and branding their cattle. To prove the falsity of the charge the following official notice is given as it was printed and sent broadcast over the country in May, 1892:

NOTICE

To Henry Blair, Dr. Harris, the Murphy Cattle Company and Other Owners of Cattle Ranging in Johnson County:

The authorities of Johnson county invite and desire that all owners of cattle ranging in this county who have either personally or by their foremen and representatives participated in the late armed invasion of this county to send able, trustworthy and discreet persons to their ranches to attend to the rounding and preservation of their property. The undersigned pledge to them the resources of the county in the protection of their interests here. We would suggest that there are a number

100

of idle cowboys here who have not been branded as outlaws or black-balled by the stock association who will gladly work and help round up the cattle during the coming season.

C. J. HOGERSON,
C. M. DEVOE,
J. T. BROWN,
County Commissioners.
ALVIN BENNETT,
County and Prosecuting Attorney.
W. G. ANGUS,
Sheriff.

Another false statement that was freely circulated throughout the country was to the effect that Johnson county was a barren waste, only suited for range cattle grazing, and that three-fourths of the taxes accrued from the range herds owned by the large cattlemen who were either present or represented in the raid. The martial law petition sent to the governor stated that the assessable value of the range herds amounted to "millions of dollars." The exact facts are presented by the county clerk in the following statement:

The assessed valuation of property in Johnson county for 1891 was $1,789,075.69. The valuation of all horses and cattle owned by stockmen was $318,125, the tax on which was $3,817.50.

This shows the cattlemen's interest in that county to have been less than one-fifth of the total, yet they claimed to be entitled to the control of all matters by reason of their money invested.

On the morning of May 10th, 1892, George A. Wellman was murdered on Nine Mile divide, in Johnson county. Here is the story as it was first told to the Bulletin, in Buffalo, on the day of the murder:

Thomas Hathaway, a cowboy, who has been for several years in the employ of H. A. Blair Company, known as the Hoe outfit, came into town Tuesday evening, unarmed, wild-eyed and excited, and unfolded a tale that created consternation among the people.

His story, as told then, is as follows:

"George A. Wellman, who, since the absence of F. H. Labertaux, was in charge of the Hoe outfit, came from Gillette to the Hoe ranch on Powder river, Monday evening, the 9th of May, paid off the men at work

there, and Tuesday morning, he (Hathaway) started with Wellman to
go to Buffalo. Each was riding a horse, and Wellman was leading a
packhorse, packed with Hathaway's bedding. When about 15 or 16 miles
southeast from the Crazy Woman stage crossing, and about 10 o'clock
in the morning, as they were riding side by side along the Nine Mile
divide, two shots were fired in quick succession, so quick that one man
could not have fired them, and George Wellman fell from his horse.

"Hathaway's horse pitched him off; he mounted again and followed
Wellman's horse and the packhorse about 300 yards to the right, stopped,
unsaddled both Wellman's horse and the packhorse, turned them loose
and rode as fast as he could to Buffalo to notify the sheriff."

Hathaway changed his story somewhat as he told it to different people, and in the evening he was arrested on suspicion
of being a party to the crime. The body was sent for and an inquest held, but no certain key to the mystery was found. The
case has been in the United States court because of the fact of
Wellman being a deputy United States marshal, but the public
is today as ignorant as it was on the morning of the murder as
to the identify of the men who fired the fatal shot. Wellman
was a popular cowboy with all the people and not known to
have an enemy in the country. The Masons of Buffalo buried
him with due honors, and general sorrow prevailed throughout
the county. He was married at Martha, Wisconsin, April 21st,
1892, had just returned from that interesting ceremony when he
was stricken down.

The belief is general in the northern counties that Wellman
died at the hands of the invaders and not by act of the so-called
rustlers. As explained in another chapter, they believe he was
selected as a victim in the hope of fastening a crime upon the
settlers of Johnson county for the purpose of exciting sympathy
for the captured white caps.

Some weeks after the discharge of the invaders Dudley Champion, a brother of Nathan, was shot and killed by Mike Shonsey,
one of the late prisoners. Champion came down the cattle trail
in search of work, and at a point about 20 miles northeast of
Lusk fell in with an outfit from Texas. During the evening meal
Shonsey rode up, and for a time pleasant conversation was carried on between the entire party. Suddenly Shonsey raised his

gun and fired, killing Champion instantly. Shonsey, accompanied by a lad who was in the employ of the Texans, immediately started for Lusk, where he gave himself up to the officers. A preliminary hearing was at once had, the boy swearing that Champion drew his revolver first, and that Shonsey fired in self-defense. This, of course, relieved Shonsey from blame, and he was released. A few hours later he took the train for Cheyenne, arriving in that city at midnight. The next morning he settled up with George W. Baxter, in whose employ he had been, and took the afternoon train south, presumably going to Mexico and out of reach of the law.

Twenty-four hours after Shonsey's release by the court at Lusk other witnesses arrived, and it was claimed that Champion had made no gun play and that his killing was unprovoked, cold-blooded murder on the part of Shonsey. But the information came too late—the murderer was flying southward and out of reach. Thus was added another crime to the long list chargeable to white cap influence.

Undoubtedly the motive for the killing of Dudley Champion was the fear that he would, if permitted to live, seek revenge for the murder of his brother Nathan at the K. C. ranch. A living Champion was looked upon as a constant menace—therefore, no Champions must be permitted to live. Shonsey is still absent from the state, and no action has been initiated to bring him back to answer for his crime.

Readers of these pages can but be impressed with the knowledge that the whole cry of the invaders and their promoters was the decimation of their herds by the rustlers. "Thief, thief!" was the constant yell, and the charge was always that, "If the thieves are not wiped out our herds will be." So they went to battle to destroy the men who had thus driven the cattle from the ranges of the state. That this was a false cry, the following story abundantly proves:

The Western Union Beef Company, of which George W. Baxter was and still is general manager, had a herd located in Johnson county, with Mike Shonsey as range foreman. The grass was short and the company had determined to move the herd to Montana in hopes of securing a better range. In the early autumn of 1892, four or five months after the invasion, the herd was gathered for the drive to Montana, and behold there were found and rounded into the moving bunches about two thousand more cattle than the company's books called for. The rustlers had not taken many of these cattle, surely. Yet, no man was a more vigorous "thief" howler than this man Baxter.

Some persons have been uncharitable enough to suggest that the general manager and the range foreman had entered into a conspiracy and "put up a job" on the company for their personal pecuniary benefit, namely, anticipating, and perhaps urging the removal of the herd, they had "doctered" the tally sheets so as to show two thousand head less than the real number. Then, when the gather was made, if they found all the books called for, less, say two or three hundred, they could buy the remnant for a few hundred dollars—less than half of the market value of the shortage, for it costs nearly all the value of the tailings of a herd to gather it—and thus have a two-thousand herd of their own. But the little unpleasantness of the invasion made the climate of Johnson county unhealthy for Messrs. Baxter and Shonsey, and the cattle gathering had to be done by cowboys not in the deal. Thus everything bearing the company's brands was brought in and the soft snap so carefully planned was "given away."

Assuming that there is no truth in this very plausible story, which is proper in the absence of direct proof, and that if Baxter and Shonsey had made the gather of the cattle, the same results would have been secured, the fact remains that the herd had not been looted, as claimed by Baxter and his co-workers in the invasion, and the belligerent attitude was assumed without cause. Baxter must accept one of the two horns of this dilemma —he either allowed the tally sheets to be incorrectly made out or he knowingly set up a false cry of stolen cattle to justify an outrage upon his state and the people such as was before unknown in the history of the United States, for no practical cattleman, as he claims to be, could visit his range month after month and year after year without realizing that his herd was rapidly increasing instead of being day by day growing less from wholesale robbery, as he everywhere proclaimed. This effectually lift the charge of cattle stealing from the citizens of Johnson county.

Several members of the Texas contingent of the invaders have paid the debt of nature since their release from custody by the Wyoming court, all dying with "their boots on;" and many of them under circumstances peculiarly distressing. One of the sad stories will be sufficient to record here. The article copied below is from the Buffalo Voice of a date early in February, 1894, under the heading, "Vengeance Is Mine:"

Last Friday, at Fort Smith, Arkansas, the Texas Kid was hung. He will be remembered as being one of the invaders, and the one who boasted that he was the man who fired the shot that killed Nick Ray. He was one of the hired Texans who got $5 a day and rations for helping Wolcott, Carey, Warren & Co. to kill and scare people out of this country in order to help out their arid land scheme. After getting out of jail he went back to Texas and murdered a girl, and for that crime he was justly hanged. He was engaged to the girl he murdered, before he came up here as an invader, and when he went back she had learned what he had done in Wyoming, and refused, not only to marry him, but told him she never wanted to see him again. He became enraged and deliberately shot her. He was soon caught, and in less than a month after committing the crime was tried and sentenced to be hung. He broke down several days before the execution of his sentence and repented of his crimes. He blamed the instigators of the invasion for being the cause of his ruin and the death of a fair, young girl. He said that he had been told by Wolcott that a band of outlaws existed in Johnson county, in comparison to whom the James boys or the Daltons were innocent children; that they not only were thieves, but that they had waylaid and killed several stockmen, and that nine out of ten of the citizens were scared to death of this gang, which numbered about 75 men. He said Wolcott and Irvine told him that the governor and both senators had offered rewards for their capture or extermination, and that the governor, as the head of the state, had given his sanction to the invasion, as had also both senators. He denounced the whole gang and expressed regret for the part he took. "Vengeance is mine, saith the Lord."

Midway between the rock-ribbed

coast of New England and the golden sands of the Pacific, high above and beyond the reach of the malaria-laden winds that gather in the low lands on either side, sits fair Wyoming, youngest born of the sons and daughters of our Republic. Resting on the summit of the great Rocky Mountains, her garments fall in graceful folds to the East and West, covering an area of nearly four hundred miles square. Within these rectangular lines is found a variety and richness of nature elsewhere unknown, and absolutely beyond the power of words or brush to paint.

Here we see the broad, treeless plains stretching away in the distance, earth and sky blending, like the sailor's morning welcome in the calm of mid-ocean. Yonder the rolling approaches to the foothills, green with grasses and decked with flowers of a thousand hues. There the foothills themselves, the body guards and picket sentinels of the great ranges, were ever on duty as the trusted soldier on the tented field. These supports to the great

106

backbone of the continent are as varied in their conformation
and consistency as are the comprehensions of the human mind.
One is the perfection of symmetry, when viewed from any quar-
ter, its sides smooth and inviting from the base to apex; another,
rock piled upon rock, craggy projections here, cavernous depths
there, walls perpendicular and walls hanging over; stones
smoothed by the action of the elements on their surfaces, or
shaped into all manner of grotesque forms by these same elements, as their composition is uniform or conglomerate in
character.

Then come the mountains, the giants in nature, rearing their
proud heads far into the ethereal blue, and from their vantage
ground wearing a smile that reaches out and gladdens the earth
in its lower fields; the dew drops from the mountains, gathered
there while the storm king reigned, are the joy, the life of the
plains below. Raised from the lower depths by the strong pulsa-
tions of nature, these mountain ranges cross the state from
south to north, with diverging spurs to the east and west, forming a network of mountains, slopes, valleys and plains. On yonder peak rest the snows of centuries, a robe of whiteness, un-
spotted by the changing rays of the sun, unsullied by the
tornado's sweep, and secure from the cyclonic embrace of elec-
tric combinations. Down the sides of this cloud-piercing pile
the pine tree grows in sturdy thrift, and from the shady nooks
spring babbling brooks that dance and sing their way to the
Platte and the Yellowstone, whence they wander on to lose
their identity in tropical seas.

The placid beauty of the plains, the enchanting, soul-inspiring
and matchless grandeur of the Platte canyon, the sublimity of
Yellowstone Park, the playground of the gods, afford a variety
of scenery so entrancing that the mind is satisfied and the soul
is filled to overflowing.

As the surface of the state invites to contemplation and satis-
fies the most ardent lover of nature's work, so beneath these
masterpieces of omnipotent mechanism lies buried a material
wealth as inexhaustible as are the sands of the sea shore. Black
diamonds, the coal of commerce, underlie more than one-half of

the state, and Wyoming could warm the nations for a century without material shrinkage of the supply. Nature's active laboratory seems to be located directly under this keystone of American commonwealths, for chemical combinations and experiments there conducted have given us not only the gems from the mountains, but pearls from the ocean depths. Every mineral of value known to commerce or manufacturers is found in greater or less quantity, and the iron mines are the marvel of all beholders. The oil fields of the state are greater than those of Pennsylvania and Ohio combined, and the soda lakes are the glory and pride of the continent.

We are blessed with the raw material for a great manufacturing community, and the soil of our valleys is like unto the delta of the Nile. The cloudless days of nearly all the year, and the bracing winds that chase o'er plain and hill drive malaria far away, and physical development becomes perfect.

Wyoming is nature's bonded warehouse. Here are stored the treasures of a continent, but for ages the doors have been securely fastened and the seals are yet unbroken. Intelligent research will find the keys and deliver the goods to a waiting world for the pleasure, comfort and enchantment of the people. To this end we invite the prospector to come within our gates and swell the number of developers.

Already blessed with a home-loving and patriotic citizenship, the topography and climatic conditions of the state will stimulate republican sentiment among all classes, and as the years and the ages roll by Wyoming will be pointed to as the birthplace of true democracy, the land of freedom to men and women, the one spot in nature's wide domain where the laws are made by the governed, without regard to sex. As we now lift our eyes to Andora, the oldest Republic, nestled securely in the fastnesses of the Pyrenees, and thank God that one tribe has preserved a republican form of government for twelve hundred years by reason of its bravery and love of human liberty, so as the history of the world's progress is written in future years, will the eyes of all people turn to this commonwealth as the land where brave men and fair women, freemen whom the truth makes free, equally hold in trust, and sacredly preserve the rights and liberties of the people.

Rocked in cradles guarded by nature's great mountain sentinels; developed in the atmosphere of freedom that breathes from every hillside and valley in these highlands; brought to man and womanhood under the magic touch of nature in its grandest forms, the offspring of Wyoming will be as proud, brave and patriotic a race as ever sprang from the descendants of Eden's illustrious pair. To a people thus fortunately situated the future is assured, and we invite the brave and the good of all lands to come and abide with us, in the full belief that the domination of the old cattle-growers' ring is ended, and that from this hour the people will rule.

CONCLUSION

With all of these natural resources and this exceptional political situation, the state is being held back in its development. Corporation rule dominated so long, and then the disgrace of the state's invasion came as a climax. Some of the invaders still hold up their heads and try to pose as men, but the dry rot has taken hold of many of them, and it is only a question of a short time until the last one will have quietly folded his tent and departed to a more congenial clime. To be pointed at with the finger of scorn by every passerby becomes wearisome, and the weariness grows oppressive. Defeat brings disgust, and as the old ring has suffered this at every turn, the practical idea of a change of pasture is already having the desired effect. From now on there will be a new Wyoming, purified by the people's rule, and made the home of a happy and prosperous population, engaged in opening up and humanizing the mountain, valley and plain.

Appendix

The following confession of George Dunning, one of the hired men of the invasion, was written by him while in the Johnson county jail, at Buffalo, duly sworn to and published in the Northwestern Livestock Journal in October, 1892. As the result of that publication the editor of the journal was arrested for criminal libel while in the city of Chicago, and his printing office seized. The postmaster at Cheyenne held all the copies of the paper containing the confession as "obscene" literature, referring the matter to the postmaster general and getting instructions (after the election) to let the paper go through the mails. Fortunately, a part of the mail left the Cheyenne office before the postmaster found out the contents of the paper, and a goodly number of copies went out by express, so that the public got the information before it quite generally.

The statements made in the confession are of a startling nature, but so many of them are known to be true that the public is disposed to accept the entire story as true in detail. The writer hereof has seen and read the original of the letters written to Dunning by H. B. Ijams, and they confirm the statements given in the confession in regard to them.

The blush of shame will come to any honest man who reads the hellish plot, as laid before Dunning, especially when he reflects that a crazy, wicked attempt was made to execute the very plans as detailed. Of course there is a good deal of superfluous verbiage used in the confession, but this is to be expected in an article prepared by an uneducated man:

CONFESSION OF GEORGE DUNNING

About the 1st of March, 1892, I was on my way from the 79 mine near Silver City, Owyhee County, Idaho, to Boise City, Idaho, which is a distance of about 60 miles. I had heard there was about to be a sale made of the 79 mine and group of mining claims; I and four other parties have a lease on the 79 mine and a group of mining claims. I was going to Boise City to see W. B. Knott, the owner of the 79 mine. I wanted to see him about getting my pay for what work I had done about the 79 mine. According to our contract with W. B. Knott we took a three-

111

years' leave on the 79 mine and group of mining claims with the understanding that if the property was sold before the expiration of our lease that each of the leasers should be paid $4 a day and all expenses for what time he worked, and each leaser was to receive $1,000 besides. When I left the mine I walked to Snake river the first day, a distance of about 30 miles, and stayed all night with a man by the name of Cox. The next morning I left Cox's place to go to the Hot Springs. As I was passing Mr. Bernard's place Mr. Bernard asked me if I had received a letter from Mr. Stearns, of Nampa. I told him I had not. Mr. Bernard said Mr. Stearns would like to see me. I asked Mr. Bernard if he knew what Mr. Stearns would like to see me about. Mr. Bernard said that Mr. Stearns would like to employ the right kind of a man to run a cow outfit in Johnson county, Wyoming, for a friend of his and that they would pay me big wages. I told Mr. Bernard that I and some other parties had a three-years' leave on the 79 mine and it had always, for the last 12 or 13 years, been considered one of the best mines in the state, and that while we were running the south drift that the ledge had lately widened out and showed higher grade rock than any other place in the mine. I told Mr. Bernard that I heard that the mine was about to be sold, and if the sale came off I would have money enough to go into something for myself, and if the sale did not come off that I should go back to the mine and get out rock so that as soon as the roads got good I could get the rock milled and get my money for it. Mr. Bernard said he heard we had a good layout on the mine, but that the man that wished to hire me and some of my friends to run his outfit of cattle was very wealthy and a member of the Wyoming Stock Growers' Association; that the association had had a good deal of trouble with their stock in Johnson county, and that the Wyoming Stock Growers' Association was the largest and wealthiest association of the kind in the world, and if I wanted to go to Wyoming to work, and if I and my friends would fill the bill that money would cut no figure with the stock association. I thought the matter over a minute or two; I was satisfied there was something wrong. I told Mr. Bernard that I would think the matter over and have a talk with Mr. Stearns; that I could see Mr. Stearns in Nampa on my way to Boise City. I then went on to the Hot Springs ranch. When I got to the Hot Springs ranch I told some of my friends that Old Bernard was up to some more of his skullduggery; that he had another scheme in view; that I did not take much stock in it, but I was going to see Mr. Stearns when I went through Nampa on my way to Boise City, and that I would learn more of the particulars. At this time I was not acquainted with Mr. Stearns. This man Bernard that I had the conversation with in regard to coming to Johnson county, Wyoming, to work was one of the leaders in the stock association in Owyhee County, Idaho, seven or eight years ago. Everything in the line of the stock business in Owyhee County, Idaho, seemed to be running smooth until the stock association was founded at

Silver City, Idaho. There was at that time little or no complaint of stock stealing in that part of the country. About the time the stock association was in working order there were rumors of cattle and horse stealing by the wholesale started around the country and men who belonged to the association said if the small stockmen did not sell out or leave the country that they would make them costs enough in court to break them up. When court set in the fall the men who belonged to the stock association kept up their howl about the amount of stealing that was going on. The sheriff of the county had turned out defaulter to a large amount of money, and in order to cover up his defalcations had committed a number of forgeries. The sheriff picked up the grand jury on the streets and managed to manipulate them in such a manner that the grand jury found two indictments against me for branding cattle, and indicted a number of other parties besides myself. The amount of money the sheriff was a defaulter was settled for him and the courts failed to convict a man that was indicted by that grand jury. This man Bernard took a very active part in the prosecution of all cattle cases. I know him personally to be a thief and a perjurer. He was continually talking about the need of a vigilance committee while the stock association was in its glory in Owyhee county, Idaho. The association only lasted about two years in Owyhee county, Idaho; it then went to wreck.

In the course of a day or so after my conversation with Mr. Bernard in regard to my coming to Johnson county to work for a cattle outfit I was in the town of Nampa, Idaho, on my way to Boise City. Mr. Stearns called to me on the streets and asked me if it would be possible for me to go to Johnson county, Wyoming, and take charge of a cattle outfit. Mr. Stearns said that it would be better if I could take four or five of my friends along; that everything would be fixed satisfactorily in regard to the money matter; that we would have a show to make some money. Mr. Stearns then went on to explain how he came to speak to me about the matter; he said he was back East on a visit last summer and he met an old friend and school chum of his by the name of Clark; said Clark was one of the best men he ever knew in his life; that Clark had made barrels of money out of the cattle business and owned a large amount of cattle in Johnson county, Wyoming, and vicinity. Mr. Stearns then went on to tell me that Clark had told him while he was back East last summer that the cattle thieves, or rustlers, were committing great depredations on his stock in Johnson county, Wyoming, and that every man they hired was standing in with the rustlers, and that things would have to take a change in Johnson county or the stockmen would have to gather up what stock they could and leave the country. Mr. Stearns said he had a talk with Mr. Clark about me and some of my friends, and told Clark that if he would give us good wages that we would run his cattle for him, and that we would run them on the square; and that it would be a cold day if Clark did not get what cattle belonged to him.

Mr. Stearns next showed me three or four telegrams that had been sent to him from Cheyenne, Wyoming, one of which read: "Please send party by next train, if possible." When I saw the telegrams there was but little doubt in my mind but what the whole business was crooked. Mr. Stearns told me that money would be forwarded to me from Cheyenne or else a man would come from Cheyenne to Nampa and explain matters, if I thought I could go to Johnson county, Wyoming. I told Mr. Stearns that I could go and to have his man, who Mr. Stearns told me would be H. B. Ijams, secretary of the Wyoming Stock Growers' Association, meet me in the course of three or four days in Nampa, Idaho. I told Mr. Stearns that I would be back from Boise City by that time. I then went to Boise City and came back to Nampa, Idaho, where I was introduced to Mr. H. B. Ijams, of Cheyenne. Mr. Ijams and I then went over to Mr. Stearns' office to have a talk about the cattle business. Mr. Ijams talked very freely about matters pertaining to the cattle business in Wyoming and especially in Johnson county. Mr. Ijams complained bitterly about the depredations he claimed that were committed upon the bands of horses and cattle by the rustlers in Johnson county and vicinity; he said that the stock growers' association would either have to put a stop to the thieves or else sell out or gather up their stock and drive them to some other state. Mr. Ijams said the stock growers' association had owned stock on the range too long to be run out of the country by an outfit of thieves, and if it was necessary the association would fight the thieves until the last one of them was wiped out of existence. Mr. Ijams said the Wyoming Stock Growers' Association had paid out thousands of dollars for hiring men from different parts of the country to kill off the horse and cattle thieves in Wyoming. Mr. Ijams said the methods of the stock association were expensive, but he knew no other way to keep the thieves down. Mr. Ijams spoke of the hanging of a man by the name of Wagoner, a horse man, and the lynching of Averill and Cattle Kate, and about the killing of Tisdale and Jones last fall and the assault on Nate Champion and his partner on Powder river last fall. Mr. Ijams said last fall the Wyoming Stock Growers' Association made a contract with certain parties to kill off 15 men who were considered by the stock association to be the leaders among the stock thieves in Johnson county, Wyoming. Mr. Ijams gave me to understand that the men who were employed by the Wyoming Stock Growers' Association to do the killing last fall in Johnson county, Wyoming, were Frank Canton and Joe Elliott and Tom Smith and another man whose name I forget, who Ijams said got off all right to Montana. Mr. Ijams said our men got Tisdale and Jones all right. The next job they tried after they attempted to do up Champion and his partner, on Powder river, they went into the Champion cabin about daylight and told Champion and his partner to give up, and at the same time one of the party fired his postol at Champion's head; Champion then shot one of the party up the coat sleeve with his revolver and another through the ribs. The party then left Champion's place, leaving their grub, blankets and several horses and overcoats in the vicinity of Champion's place. Mr. Ijams said that the failure of their men to do up Champion and his partner, on Powder river, and the killing of Tisdale and Jones last fall put an end to the killing business for the rest of the winter in Johnson county.

Mr. Ijams said that after the assault on Champion and his partner and the killing of Tisdale and Jones last fall, on the Powder river, there was a good deal of excitement in Johnson county, and people were getting on the war path; that the stock association thought that if they had some of the thieves killed off that it would terrorize the balance in such a manner that the most of them would leave the country. Mr. Ijams said the stock association were mistaken in regard to the effect produced by the killing off of a few thieves by men who were hired by the stock association; that instead of terrorizing the rascals that the thieves were becoming more bold in committing their depredations upon livestock, and that the thieves were getting more on the war path every day of their rascally lives. Mr. Ijams said that the course the stock association had been pursuing for a number of years in regard to killing off the thieves in Johnson county and vicinity had bitterly prejudiced a great many ranchers and business men and other people who never owned any stock, against the stock association; that he had thought the matter over a great deal and had lately come to the conclusion that the stock association had not gone about the killing off of the thieves in the right manner. Mr. Ijams said that since the assault on Champion and his partner and the killing of Tisdale and Jones, on Powder river, last fall that the stock association had another scheme in view for doing up the thieves and he thought it was the proper one under the circumstances, and that this last scheme would meet the approbation of a great many law-abiding citizens of Johnson county, who would shudder at the idea of the stock association hiring men in Cheyenne or Texas to come to Johnson county to shoot the cattle thieves in the back. Mr. Ijams said that the latest scheme of the stock association was to publicly wipe the thieves in Johnson county, Wyoming, out of existence; the way he said the stock association of Montana did in that state eight or nine years ago. Mr. Ijams said that after the assault on Champion and the killing of Jones and Tisdale, that one of the stock association's best men, a man by the name of Tom Smith, had gone to Texas to get 25 men to join the rest of the outfit in Cheyenne whenever the stock association saw fit to make a raid on Johnson county and kill off the thieves; said Smith used to be a deputy United States marshal in Texas; and that a number of deputy United States marshals would come from Texas with Smith. Ijams said Smith had been engaged in the business of killing off cattle thieves for a number of years, and was the most successful man he knew of in his line of business. Ijams said Smith was the man who put up the job to hang a horseman named Wagoner. Ijams said Smith and party read a bogus warrant to Wagoner and took him a short distance from home and hanged him. Mr. Ijams said the stock association were hiring the men that Smith would bring from Texas on the basis of $5 a day for each man hired and all expenses would be paid by the association; and the association would pay each hired man $50 for every man that was killed or hung by the mob on the raid. Ijams said that most of the work would be accomplished in a month, but he intended to divide the mob up after the first month's work and have five men in each squad, and have them ride over the country for several months and kill the thieves whenever they run on them. Mr. Ijams said the mob would probably kill off about 30 men in Johnson county while on their raid; that the stock association wanted to kill off more, but that a good many thieves would escape. After the mob got through with Johnson county they were to visit other parts of the country. Mr. Ijams said the mob would have three or four months' work and it might take them all summer. When the mob got through with Wyoming, Ijams said the association had raids planned for other parts of the country. Ijams said the stock association had 25 or 30 friends in Buffalo and vicinity who would join the mob when they got in the vicinity of Buffalo; said the friends of the stock association in Buffalo were determined men, and that the mayor of the town (a man I believe by the name of Burritt) was at the head of their organization. Ijams said the governor and Judge Blake were back of this movement to wipe the thieves in Johnson county out of existence. Ijams told me about the United States marshal helping him plan the raid and said that the stock association had some very warm friends in Congress and the United States Senate, among whom he said was Senator Carey, a man of great influence and wealth. Ijams spoke about the sheriff and his deputies in Johnson county, and said they were in sympathy with the cattle thieves, and that he would rather have the sheriff and one of his deputies, a man I believe by the name of Rowles, hung than any two s— of b— he knew of. Ijams spoke of Rowles as the affidavit fiend; said Rowles had caused the stock association a good deal of trouble by getting out affidavits against some of the parties the stock association had employed to kill off the cattle thieves in Johnson county. Mr. Ijams said the stock association had a great many influential friends all over Wyoming; he said the association paid no attention to the courts in Johnson county; that all the courts were on their side; he spoke about Frank Canton being arrested for killing Jones and Tisdale, and said the evidence was very strong against Canton, but that Canton's friends were obliged to prove an alibi for him; said the affidavits in regard to Canton's proving an alibi had been gotten up to fit the case, and were false as far as the truth of the matter was concerned; that it was no trouble for the stock association to procure affidavits to fit any case. Ijams said that if the raid came off that it would come off before the cattle round-up; he said that when about 30 of the thieves were killed off that 300 or 400 people who were in sympathy with the thieves would get up and leave the country the best way they could; that the people who were in sympathy with the thieves would leave their stock on the range; that before the raid was over the stock association would have a round-up of the cattle in Johnson county and take possession of all the cattle on the range that belonged to the cattle thieves and their sympathizers; that the stock association would ship the beef and brand over the rest of the rustlers' cattle. Ijams said that if I and my friends were willing to work with the mob on the same terms that the stock association were hiring the rest of the mob in Texas that the stock association would be glad to have us join the mob in Cheyenne at some future time. I told Ijams that I thought his terms were very liberal. Ijams said there would be no trouble about any of the mob getting their money according to contract. I told Ijams that I was willing to take the stock association for my pay. Ijams said it had not been definitely settled yet just when the mob would leave Cheyenne or just what action the stock association would take about the matter. Ijams said it would be necessary for him to return immediately to Cheyenne and confer with two other men who were officers in the stock association, who, with him, had the management of affairs in regard to recruiting a mob of men to come to Johnson county, Wyoming, and kill off the cattle thieves. Ijams said his propositions to me were made as an agent of the Wyoming Stock Growers' Association. And before the association knew just what they would do about the matter it would be necessary for the association to hold a meeting at their headquarters in Cheyenne, and before the mob could start from Cheyenne to Johnson county, Wyoming, to kill off the cattle thieves, that it would be necessary at the stock association meeting for every member of the association or his representative to endorse the general plan of campaign of Ijams and the other two officers of the association who were connected with the recruiting of the mob to come to Johnson county, Wyoming, for the purpose of killing off the cattle thieves and rustlers. Mr. Ijams said he would write me a letter once in a while after he got back to Cheyenne and keep me posted in regard to affairs. I then left Ijams in Nampa and went to Caldwell, nine miles west of Nampa. This interview I had with Ijams in Nampa, Idaho, was on the 7th of March, 1892. Before I left Ijams in Nampa I asked him what was the general reputation of the cattle thieves and rustlers in Johnson county in the neighborhood where they lived. Ijams said the thieves the stock association intended to have killed off generally bore a good reputation in Johnson county and vicinity where they lived. Ijams said they were not generally considered thieves or outlaws in Johnson county and vicinity.

After my arrival in Caldwell I did not know hardly how to regard Ijams' proposition. Ijams was perfectly sober at the time of our interview and seemed to be a very intelligent kind of a man. I saw Ijams talking in Nampa to one of the head men of the Ada County Stock Association, a man by the name of Valentine. I thought the matter over a good deal. Ijams did not seem to get mad or excited during our conversation in Nampa, but seemed to talk about the matter of murdering 30 or more men in much the same manner that many people would talk about taking a picnic excursion. I could not think for some time that Ijams was in earnest, he seemed to have other business in the county besides interviewing me. Ijams asked me if I knew a man by the name of Lamb, in Silver City, Idaho, that used to be editor of the Silver City Avalanche, and wanted to know if Lamb was in Silver City or vicinity. I told him that Lamb was in Delamar, Idaho, about nine miles from Silver City. Ijams said that he once loaned Lamb $1,500 in St. Louis and that Lamb had never returned the money. Ijams said he had a notion to go to Silver City and see Lamb. Ijams inquired about Lamb's ability to pay the $1,500 and gave up the trip. I was satisfied that Ijams and some of those fellows in Nampa were trying to give me a talk on the side to see if I would not have Ijams arrested in Nampa, Idaho, or make a fool out of myself in some other way. Ijams while in Nampa had shown me a list of the men he wanted killed in Johnson county, Wyoming. Ijams spoke about three of the Ninemeier brothers who had killed three men at Silver Mountain, Idaho, and said they had been recommended to him as the right kind of men for his business. The governor of Idaho had offered $1,500 each for the capture of the Ninemeier brothers that murdered the three men in Silver Mountain, Idaho.

When I was at Caldwell waiting to get paid for my work about the 79 mine I thought over Ijams' proposition a good deal. I could not conceive how any one had any reason to think that I and my friends were so diabolically inclined as to join a mob and go to a distant part of the country and engage in the business of murdering men by wholesale who stood in the same position before the Wyoming Stock Growers' Association that I and my friends a few years ago did to the Owyhee County Stock Association in Idaho. I and my friends in Idaho are about the only ones that ever had any trouble with the stock association in Owyhee county, Idaho. The stock association dealt us a good deal of aggravation for nearly two years, a large amount of which was blackmail, and some of the wretches had not quit lying the last I heard from them. While the stock association was in existence in Owyhee county, I took a very active part in dealing the institution misery. I and my friends took a very active part in prosecuting and trying to bring to justice some of the perjurers and assassins whom we claim were in the employ of the stock association. I have gone to a good deal of trouble and expense in Idaho to work a hardship upon that misguided and unfortunate institution of a stock association during its short and melancholy existence in Owyhee county, Idaho. The more I thought of Ijams' propositions the more I became convinced that Ijams had been imposing on me with his stories in regard to killing off the cattle thieves in Johnson county, Wyoming. When the members of the Owyhee County Stock Association in Idaho were talking unusually wicked and seemed to be thirsting for gore, I and some of my friends formed an association for the purpose of bringing to justice any of the members of the stock association who should do a small stockman an injustice. And we intended to bring to justice any criminals that might be in the employ of the stock association, and we were quite successful in running down some of the criminals in the employ of the stock association. Our association was an organization for the mutual protection of the small stockmen. We were to brand each other's stock when convenient and favor each other in other ways. Our association I have every reason to believe is in as good running order today as it ever was. We call it the Owyhee and Bruneau Stock Association. Soon after my interview with Ijams in Nampa, Idaho, I saw a friend of mine in Caldwell by the name of Henry Dement, who was a member of our organization, for running down vigilantes or criminals in the employ of the stock association of Owyhee county, Idaho. I spoke to Dement about the propositions that Ijams had made to me in Nampa; Dement said it would be a good idea for me to keep my eyes open; that the stock association was strong in Wyoming, and it was hard telling what they would do in that country. After I saw Dement I thought the matter over a good deal and came to the conclusion that as far as Ijams' proposition to me was concerned, that the whole business was a fake. I could not conceive how Ijams could imagine that I and my friends were composed of the right material for a mob. I could not think of any circumstance that any of us had ever been accused of that would justify Ijams in arriving at his conclusions. After a couple of weeks I got two letters from Ijams, saying he would keep me informed when he wanted me and party to start for Cheyenne, and he would let me know the number of men to bring with me. When I had my first interview with Ijams I knew nothing about any of the troubles in Johnson county, Wyoming. After I got my second letter from Ijams I began to pay some attention to his stories. After I got my second letter from Ijams I went to Boise City to see about getting my pay for my work about the 79 mine; on my way to Boise City and in Boise City I met several men who had lately come from Johnson county or vicinity. I inquired about the state of affairs in Johnson county in regard to the cattle business. One of these men I had a talk with was Bob Gunnall, a noted foot-racer, and bartender at the Wilson Hotel in Nampa, Idaho. Gunnall said he was just from Johnson county and vicinity; came from there about six months ago. Gunnall told me about the killing of Jones and Tisdale, and about the state of affairs generally in Johnson county,

Wyoming. Gunnall was very bitter against the Wyoming Stock Growers' Association, and said the association had spent thousands of dollars for the purpose of hiring professional assassins in Texas and other places to come to Johnson county, Wyoming, and vicinity and shooting law-abiding people in the back. Gunnall said the people of Johnson county were wild with excitement on account of the murders that had been committed upon peaceable and law-abiding citizens in Johnson county by assassins in the employ of the Wyoming Stock Growers' Association. Gunnall spoke well of the people of Johnson county and vicinity; said that as a rule they were as law-abiding a class of people as could be found anywhere; that he believed there was less stock stealing going on in Johnson county than there was in most any county anywhere where there was as much stock as there was in Johnson county. I asked Gunnall if he did not think the stock association would attempt at some time to hang up some of the people of Johnson county the way the stock association of Montana hung up the so-called thieves in that state eight or nine years ago. Gunnall said it would be just as good a thing as the people of Johnson county would want for the stock association to turn a mob loose in Johnson county; that a mob of 2,000 men could not intimidate the people of Johnson county. The other men I saw and had conversations with seemed to have about the same idea about matters in Johnson county, Wyoming, that Gunnall did; they all spoke of the people as a law-abiding class of people, and all agreed that the Wyoming Stock Growers' Association of Cheyenne had been importing assassins from Texas and other places to Wyoming for the purpose of shooting people from ambush whom the stock association styled rustlers or cattle thieves. After I had my conversation with Gunnall and others in regard to the cattle business in Johnson county and vicinity, I began to think that Ijams might have been in earnest to a certain extent in regard to his propositions to me. I was convinced of the utter hopelessness and foolishness for the stock association to ever send a mob to Johnson county, if Ijams meant anything by his propositions to me. I supposed he meant to recruit an outfit of men and have them go to work in Johnson county in his cow outfit, and then see, after he was well acquainted with his men, how many men he could select out of the outfit that were of the same stripe that Frank Canton had been represented to me to be. I began to think Ijams was in earnest. I stayed in Boise City several days and tried to get my pay for my work in the 79 mine, and tried to get money from other sources, and spoke to some of my friends, Henry Dement and Frank Speelman, about rustling money for one of them to come to Johnson county, Wyoming, and let certain parties know about Ijams' proposition to me. I could not get the money to send a man ahead in time to inform the authorities in regard to Ijams' propositions to me. It did not used to be any trouble for me to borrow a few hundred dollars in Idaho. I most always had money when I was engaged in the cattle business. But during the last few years that I have been mining and doing other work, I have gone broke on pretty nearly every project I have tackled. I had $1,484 coming to me for my work about the 79 mine; I have not got any of the money yet; I soaked my revolver in Caldwell in a pawn shop to get money to go to Boise City on, and try to rustle money in order to send a man ahead to let certain parties in Johnson county know what propositions Ijams had been making to me; I never got my six-shooter out of soak until Ijams sent me the money to come to Cheyenne. I left the letters that Ijams sent me with Henry Dement, of Caldwell, Idaho. I talked the whole matter over with Dement and others, so that if the mob came into Johnson county or were captured on the way they could not make any bull story stick in regard to their coming to Johnson county with peaceable intentions. Ijams always represented to me that the first thing the stock association had to do was to kill off the rustlers and then the stock association would have a round-up of the cattle in Johnson county before the mob left the county, and that the stock association would appropriate all of the rustlers' cattle and horses and all stock that belonged to the sympathizers of the rustlers. Before I left Idaho I tried to get Bob Gunnall to come to Cheyenne with me. I was satisfied from what I heard that Gunnall was well acquainted in Cheyenne and had relations living there who were well fixed and could let Gunnall have the money to come ahead and inform the authorities in Johnson county in case we had reason to believe that the outfit that was to leave Cheyenne was a mob and were coming to Johnson county with the intention of killing off the rustlers. I told Gunnall that I was confident that we would capture enough of the criminals in Cheyenne to pay us handsomely on account of certain parties I expected would be in Cheyenne with the mob about the time we got there that had large rewards offered for their capture. Gunnall said he would like to come, but I would make it all right any way, and that he was badly in debt in Nampa and could not leave the country until he squared up; that he had to go to Delamar right away and run a foot race; that it would be $1,200 or $1,500 in his pocket to run the race.

I arrived in Cheyenne, April 2nd, 1892; I came in on the 5 o'clock afternoon train; I was in town five or ten minutes when I met Ijams on the street; he said he was just looking around and was expecting to see me and a party from Idaho. He asked me how many men I had brought along with me; I told him that I was obliged to come alone this trip, as I and my friends were expecting a good deal of trouble in my part of the country, and it would be necessary for every one of my friends to get to the front if matters took the turn that we expected they would; he said that we would get along nicely any way; that Smith had no trouble in getting the number of men in Texas that he wanted at the rates the stock association offered, $5 a day wages and all expenses paid by the association, and $50 bounty to be paid to each hired man for every man that was killed in the raid made by the mob in Johnson county or vicinity. I said that the terms were the same as we had talked about at Nampa; Ijams asked me if the terms on which the stock association had hired the men in Texas were satisfactory to me. I told him I thought the terms of the association were very liberal. He said if I chose to remain in the country after the raid that the stock association would be able to offer other inducements to me. He then asked me if I had brought my bedding and saddle or my guns. I told him that I brought nothing with me but my revolver. He said that he would go around town with me tomorrow and show me the stores where the stock association generally did their trading, and he would make arrangements for me to get anything I needed in my line, and have it charged to the stock association. Ijams said he would have plenty of time, that we could not start as soon as he thought we would when he sent me the letter to Caldwell. Ijams said the stock growers' association had not held their meeting yet, and that the men from Texas would not come from Denver until the Wyoming Stock Growers' Association had held their meeting. Ijams said the coming meeting of the Wyoming Stock Growers' Association would be the most important meeting of the kind ever held in this Western country. Ijams said it would be necessary for every member of the Wyoming Stock Growers' Association to be present at the next meeting or to be represented by proxy, and that it would be necessary for every one of them to endorse the general plan of campaign of Ijams and two other officers of the association who had charge of the arrangements for recruiting a mob of men for the purpose of coming to Johnson county, Wyoming, and killing off the rustlers. Ijams then asked me if I had a hotel that suited me. He said I could stop at the Inter-Ocean or the Metropolitan, and that the stock association would settle my bill; he said that there were a number of stockmen who were going on the raid to pilot the mob through the country stopping at those two hotels. I told Ijams that I had on my working clothes and I would rather stop at some cheaper hotel. He said all right, to suit myself, to knock around town and enjoy myself the best I knew how, and if I wanted a suit of clothes or money I could have them, and that I would want to get me a good rig, that I was now working for a rich firm and that at the figures I would get for my work that it would not take me long to pay for a good outfit, and that one average killing for the mob would pay for a first-class rig and probably more. Ijams and I then parted; I went over to the Dyer house, a 25-cent hotel, and registered my name. After supper, about 8 o'clock in the evening, I met Ijams and two other men on the streets; Ijams introduced the two men to me as Mr. Morrison and Mr. Tabor. He said Morrison and Tabor would show me around the town. I had a long conversation with Morrison and Tabor that evening. They said they had been in the employ of the stock association for a number of years as stock detectives; they said they had worked for the stock association so long that the association thought they owned them. They said they were going along with the rest of the mob when they left Cheyenne to go to Johnson county to kill off the rustlers. They said the mob would first come to Buffalo and kill off what men they wanted in town, that they would shoot or hang up the sheriff and his deputies and would depose the civil authorities and keep possession of the town until the stock growers' association could have their own officers to take charge of the courts of Johnson county. They said the mob would have to do a good deal of fighting in Johnson county; but when the mob cleaned up Johnson county that it would raid Natrona, Sheridan and Converse counties, and would meet with little opposition in those counties and in the Sweetwater county; that the rustlers outside of Johnson county were unprepared to make a fight, and were not expecting anything, and that all the mob would have to do would be to hang them up as they come to them. Morrison and Tabor said the mob would have its hands full in Johnson county; that last fall the Wyoming stock growers had employed four men to kill off a number of rustlers; that these four men made an assault on a man by the name of Champion and Gilbertson, on the Powder river; said these four men intended to hang Champion and Gilbertson in their cabin; that they went into the cabin about daylight and told Champion and Gilbertson to give up, that they had got them this time; that while these four men were holding their revolvers on Champion and Gilbertson that Champion got his revolver and shot one of the party up the coat sleeve and the other through the short ribs; that the party then retreated leaving their horses, overcoats, bedding, some grub and a Winchester that Tom Smith had at one time made Frank Canton a present of. I understood Morrison to say that the parties to the assault on Champion and Gilbertson were Frank Canton, Joe Elliott, Tom Smith and Fred Coats; they said that last fall after the assault on Champion and Gilbertson, that there were two men killed near Buffalo by the name of Jones and Tisdale; they said that the party that killed Jones and Tisdale was in the employ of the stock association; they said that Champion and others knew who these men were that were in the employ of the stock association, and that the mob would do all witnesses up that knew of any facts that would tend to criminate any of the parties who had been in the employ of the association for the purpose of killing off the rustlers; they said the stock association had offered these four men in their employ for the purpose of killing off the rustlers $1,500 for each man killed. They asked me what arrangements I had made with Ijams in regard to my wages during the raid of the mob in Johnson county. I told them I had not made any definite arrangements yet, but that I would work the same as the rest of the mob. They said that the Stock Growers' Association had told them that they were hiring the Texas men on the basis of $5 a day wages and all expenses paid by the association, and $50 bounty to be paid to each hired man of the outfit for every man that was killed by the mob; they said the stock association told them they would give them the same rates, but if any of the mob were getting more, that they wanted the limit; that they did not want to work cheaper than the rest of the mob on account of their having been in the employ of the stock association for a number of years. Tabor said he was in the Powder river country, in Johnson county, last fall; that the men who were in the employ of the stock association for the purpose of killing off the rustlers had terrorized Johnson county to such an extent that everybody carried Winchesters and six-shooters wherever they went, and that when the settlers were going to Buffalo, if they were on horseback, that they hardly ever traveled the main roads, and that they always tried to ride around the gulches and bunches of brush. Tabor said the settlers seemed to think that the stock association had a man hired to stand behind every bunch of brush or rock in the country for the purpose of taking their scalps for the bounty that was offered by the stock association. Tabor said his business in Johnson county was looking out the country and keeping cases on rustlers. He said that a liquor or dry goods drummer could not come into Buffalo without the settlers thinking that he was in the employ of the stock association and had his valises loaded with dynamite for the purpose of blowing them up.

This is the substance of my interview with Morrison and Tabor the first night I was in Cheyenne.

On the morning of the 3rd of April I met Ijams on the street; I told him that I was looking around town to see about getting me a Winchester. He said he had just bought me one that morning, a 45-90 Browning Brothers' patent. He said the outfit would get all their guns at one store, and that the stock association would foot the bill. I went over to the store to look at my gun. I saw a number of stockmen getting guns and ammunition, among whom were H. W. Davis, D. R. Tisdale, J. N. Tisdale and others. The next day I got me a saddle and the rest of my rig. The day I got my gun I saw a man in the gun store April 3rd, when I was looking at my gun. His name was Fred Wombold. He said he used to scout for the government with a man by the name of Ketchum, brother of the man that was lynched by the Olive outfit in Nebraska. We had a long talk about mob law generally, and Wombold said he had been watching things around the gun shop, and that the stockmen had already bought over 20 guns there that day, and that they were organizing a mob to come to Johnson county to kill off the rustlers. I told Wombold when the mob would leave Cheyenne. He gave me to understand that he would come ahead of the mob and inform the authorities in Johnson county. There was a good deal of excitement at the gun store when the mob got their guns. Ben Morrison and Tabor told me that the whole town was onto the racket of the mob going to Johnson county. They said that all the officials in Cheyenne were friends of the stock associa-

tion, and we would not be molested on that account. I asked them if the
soldiers were not liable to hold up the train when the mob got opposite
Fort Russell. They said that Governor Barber had the running of the
soldiers and he would not allow them to molest the mob; that Barber
had helped plan the raid the mob was about to make, and that the officers
at Fort Russell were friends of the stockmen.

On the evening of the 3rd of April I got acquainted with a man by
the name of Mike Burns from Buffalo. We had a long talk about the
mob; he told me he would start for Buffalo on the morning train and
would inform the authorities in regard to the mob. On the 4th of April
I helped to brand the horses that the mob left Cheyenne with; there
were three carloads of them; they were branded AL on the left shoulder.
When we were branding horses I was introduced to Joe Elliot, Van
Tassal, Ewing, Clark and others. When we were branding horses there
was a good deal of talk about the state of terror the settlers of Johnson
county were in on account of the depredations that had been committed
upon the settlers by Elliott, Canton, Tom Smith and Fred Coats. There
was a good deal of talk about the necessity of killing off all men who
were witnesses against Elliott, Canton, Tom Smith and Coats. These
were the four men that it was claimed were in the employ of the Wyoming Stock Association for the purpose of killing off the rustlers last
fall. It seemed to be the general opinion among the gang at the stock
yards that if the mob could kill off about 30 rustlers in Johnson county
that it would terrorize the settlers in such a manner that 300 or 400
settlers that owned stock and were in sympathy with the rustlers,
would leave the country the best way they could, and the stock association would have no trouble about appropriating their stock, together
with the stock of the rustlers the mob intended to kill.

On the 5th day of April I helped to load the three wagons and the
three carloads of horses, and the baggage that belonged to the mob; a
man by the name of Van Tassal bossed the job. I saw Ijams again on
the afternoon of the 5th of April. He said the Wyoming Stock Association had held their meeting; he said the stock association had approved
of the general plan of the campaign of his (Ijams) and the other two
officers of the stock association who had charge of the arrangements
for recruiting the mob and of the general plan of killing the rustlers.
He said the mob would get along nicely; that every man that was a
member of the Wyoming Stock Growers' Association was backing up
the movement; that Governor Barber, Judge Blake, the United States
marshal and nearly all the state officials were on the side of the stock
association, and would stay with the mob through thick and thin. He
said the mob had some very influential friends in Congress and in the
United States Senate, among whom he said were Senators Carey and
Warren, whom he said were men of great influence and wealth. I asked
Ijams if he thought the outfit might not be arrested at Fort Russell on

the way to Casper. He said there was no danger; that Governor Barber and Senators Warren and Carey would manipulate the troops; that the troops could not be called out except for the protection of the mob, and that the mob would be able to take care of itself, and that the officers at Fort Russell were friends of the stockmen. I asked Ijams how about the troops at Buffalo. He said the troops at Buffalo were an outfit of sons of b—; that they had been stealing beef from the stockmen for years, and that the officers at McKinney upheld them in committing their depredations; that the soldiers at McKinney would invest the amount they saved by not drawing beef rations in luxuries, and the soldiers at McKinney were able to eat pluff duff three times a day.

Ijams said that arrangements had been made to watch the soldiers very closely at McKinney and see that they did not desert or steal a Gatling gun and join the rustlers. He said that parties in Buffalo would look after the soldiers so closely at McKinney that they would be perfectly harmless so far as the mob was concerned. About 6 o'clock in the evening the mob left on the train for Casper. Before leaving the stockyards the mob in Cheyenne were joined by the mob from Texas that came on the train from Denver. I think there were about 52 men on the train when the mob left Cheyenne. There was no excitement on the train until after dark, when orders were given for every man to get a rope and to have his guns ready. The leaders of the mob said the sheriff from Buffalo and one or two of his deputies might be coming on the train from Casper to Cheyenne; that a good many people in Cheyenne had known for some time the mob would start for Johnson county and that the people in Buffalo might have heard about the mob, and the sheriff and one or two deputies might be coming to Cheyenne to see what they could find out. The leaders of the mob said arrangements had been made so the mob would know if the sheriff and party were on the train, and if they were they said it would change the plans of the mob altogether. That it would be necessary for the mob to stop the train from Casper if the sheriff and party were on and to hang the sheriff and his deputies and any rustlers that might be on the train. The leaders of the mob said there were several rustlers in Casper that they would hang up if they were obliged to capture the sheriff and party from Buffalo, but if sheriff and party were not on the train from Casper that the mob would go direct to Buffalo without interfering with any one. Before the train the mob was on met the train from Casper the leaders of the mob reported that sheriff and party were not on the train from Casper. The train the mob was on arrived at the stockyards near Casper a short time before daylight and commenced to catch and saddle up their horses. By the time the part of the mob left the stockyards that had their horses in the last of the three cars the sun was about one-half or three-fourths of an hour high, and parties in Casper seemed to be watching the mob closely. Some of the mob said there were several rustlers in Casper from Johnson county that they ought to hang, but they did not want to make any disturbance until they got to Buffalo. They said if the mob caused a disturbance in Casper the sheriff in Buffalo would swear in 100 or 200 deputies and come to meet the mob in the Powder river country. The mob said the only way they could succeed was to come to Buffalo and kill off the sheriff and his deputies, so that the citizens would have no leader and no law in the country to protect them. The mob came about six or seven miles north of Casper and stopped for the wagons to come up in order to get breakfast. The mob stopped in camp until about 1 o'clock. About noon several of the mob went out and brought in a horseman. The mob said they intended to kill all rustlers that they would capture on the road. They held the horseman prisoner for about half an hour. He was unarmed and proved to be a man that was riding after sheep. They took him along prisoner for six or seven miles north of where they camped at noon and turned him loose, after making him promise to say nothing about seeing the mob in the country. The first night out from Casper, the night of the 6th of April, the mob camped about 20 miles north of Casper. On the morning of the 7th of April they were called together and told that hereafter the Texas part of the mob would be in command of Tom Smith, and the rest of them would be in command of Frank Canton; for them to obey orders and ask no questions. About 10 o'clock on the morning of the 7th of April the mob stopped a young man from Buffalo by the name of Kingsbury. They said he was a sheep man's son. He was allowed to go his way. About noon on the 7th of April they camped about 30 miles north of Casper and got dinner. From there they left the wagons and arrived at John Tisdale's on the night of the 7th of April about 8 o'clock in the evening, the weather was very stormy. About 10 or 12 miles before the mob got to Tisdale's ranch they were met by Mike Shonsey, who informed them that at a ranch on Powder river there were 15 or 16 rustlers. I could not get any information at the time just what ranch it was the rustlers were at, or in just what part of the country the ranch was, but I have since learned that the ranch that Shonsey meant was the K. C. ranch, on the middle fork of Powder river. The Texas part of the mob stopped in the bunk-house at Tisdale's ranch; the stockmen stopped at the residence. I was with the Texas party. On the morning of the 8th of April we were told by the leaders of the mob that we would lay over at Tisdale's place that day and wait for the wagons to come up and the men would have a chance to rest. The Texas men were about played out. In the afternoon we were told that the leaders had decided to make a raid on the rustlers on Powder river, about 16 miles from Tisdale's. The leaders in the evening gave orders for the mob to kill every man on this ranch they proposed to raid, and to leave no man alive about the ranch to tell any tales afterwards, no matter who he might be. The wagons arrived at Tisdale's ranch about 5 o'clock the evening of the 8th of April.

After the wagons arrived at Tisdale's we were told by the leaders that it would be the last place we would probably see the wagons unless by an accident the teamsters were able to deceive the rustlers and get through to Buffalo; that for every man to get what ammunition and blankets he wanted to take along with him; that after raiding the ranch on the Powder river the country would be full of straggling rustlers, and the chances were they would capture the wagons. About 7 o'clock in the evening four men were detailed to go to the ranch on Powder river and keep off a safe distance and see if the parties who lived at the ranch had left or not. I managed to get one of the Texans, who was detailed for the occasion, to let me go in his place. I had caught my horse and started to saddle up, when Wolcott came down from the house and said I could not go along with the party to investigate matters. He said the men that were detailed for the occasion would have to go, and that us fellows would have to learn to obey orders better and ask less questions. If I had gone along with the party of four to investigate matters at the K. C. ranch I intended when we got in sight of the K. C. ranch to get off my horse and empty my Winchester at the rest of the gang and then to go down to the house and inform the parties who were living there as to the state of affairs in their part of the country. Mike Shonsey, Jack Jones, Elick Kinzie and one of the Bookers left Tisdale's ranch to investigate matters at the K. C. ranch, on the middle fork of Powder river. They were to meet the balance of us four miles south of K. C. ranch, after they had investigated matters and let the rest of the mob know how everything was running about the ranch.

The mob left Tisdale's ranch about 11 o'clock on the night of the 8th of April and stopped several hours in a gulch on the road about four miles from K. C. ranch and waited for the return of Shonsey and party. Shonsey and their party finally returned to the gulch where the balance of the mob were waiting, and reported everything all right at the K. C. ranch; they said the parties there were not expecting anything, and that they were playing the fiddle and having a good time generally. Shortly after the return of Shonsey and party the mob started for the K. C. ranch. Joe Elliott had about 10 pounds of giant powder tied behind his saddle. It was the intention of the mob to blow the house at the K. C. ranch up with the giant powder and to shoot any of the men who showed up in sight at the K. C. house after the explosion. But the mob got to the K. C. ranch too late to use the powder. It was breaking day when we got in sight of the ranch; about the time the mob saw the K. C. house the leaders of the mob, Major Wolcott, Frank Canton and Tom Smith, called the mob to halt, pointed out to the K. C. house and said the parties they proposed to kill were living there and that they did not intend to allow any man that was about the place to get away alive. They said the mob were too late to use the giant powder; that they would have to surround the house and let the parties come out as far as possible and then they would shoot them down. The leaders then ordered six men to go on the south side of the K. C. house and conceal themselves in a gulch in order to shoot any parties that might show up in sight. The six men ordered to take a position in a gulch south of the K. C. house were Mike Shonsey, Jack Jones, Elick Kinzie and three of the Bookers. The balance of the mob went to the river and left their horses in charge of a part of the mob at the river about one-half mile above the house; a part of the balance of the mob went down the river from where they left the horses and hid behind the bank of the river for a distance of about 100 yards above the bridge, and the rest of the mob went to the stable, and some of them were concealed in the stable and to the left of the stable; and some of the mob were behind the end of the stable next to the river. When daylight come John Tisdale and I noticed a wagon in front of the K. C. house; Tisdale said that the party at the house had company.

I told Tisdale that the vistors might be friends of the stockmen who were travelling through the country, and were obliged to stop all night at the ranch. I told Tisdale that I did not hire out to kill men as I came to them, and I thought it would be a good idea if we found out who the strangers were at the K. C. house. Tisdale said he would like to find out who the parties were, but it would not be safe to go to the house. I told Tisdale that I would take chances on going to the house; that I would go a-foot and tell the parties at the house that I came from Buffalo and was going to the railroad to leave the country. Tisdale said all right, for me to go to the stable and tell the men at the stable about it. I went to the stable and told Canton and Wolcott that Tisdale was satisfied that the parties at the house were friends of his, and that he told me to go to the house and investigate. Wolcott and Canton said that Tisdale must be crazy; that they would allow no man to go to the house; that if the parties at the house were friends of his that the chances were they would be out of luck. If I had gone to the house I intended to inform the parties at the house about the mob, and I intended to stop at the house and not return. I was satisfied with what Joe Elliott and others had told me that the mob could never dislodge the parties in the house. I never heard them say anything about running a wagon against a house to burn it down, but I was afterwards told that the plan was studied up in Cheyenne over a year before the mob started. After my talk with Wolcott and Canton about going to the house, I went back along the river bank to where I had left Tisdale. Orders had been given by the leaders for every man to carry but five cartridges in his six-shooter and to have no loads in his Winchester; it was claimed that at the time that Joe Elliott and party made the assault on Champion and Gilbertson, that the party were waiting in the brush for Champion and Gilbertson to come out of the house so they could shoot them, and that one of the party let his six-shooter fall on the ground, and that it went off, and the party were obliged to make an assault on them for fear they might have heard the gun and would get to thinking the matter over and would not come out of the house. The leaders said that if any of the gang did not want their heads shot off they had better not allow any guns to go off accidentally. The mob lay in ambush at least two hours before any one showed up at the house; then one man came out and went back into the house again. In about 15 minutes afterwards an old man came out of the house with a water bucket in his hand and came straight towards the river. I kept showing up all that I thought was necessary, when I saw the two men appear, but the old man kept coming right straight for the river. When he had got behind the bank of the river Frank Canton, Joe Elliott, Ben Morrison, Tom Tabor and Tom Smith took the old man prisoner and had one of the Texas kids guard him down in under the river bank, just below the bridge. In about half an hour after the capture of the old man two men came out of the house and seemed to be on the lookout from their appearance. I thought they were aware there was something wrong. I kept dodging up so they could see me, and the largest man of the two went in the house in a rush.

And the young fellow stood around awhile and seemed to be watching in the direction of the river. I showed up again in sight. The bank was poor protection where I was. The young fellow had just gone in the house and I expected they would begin shooting from the house. I left my position and went up the river about 40 yards to where John Tisdale was at a cottonwood tree. The young fellow showed up again and came out of the house and picked up a club and began whittling on it and coming toward the river. He seemed to be on the lookout all the time. It took him about half an hour to come from the house to the stable. He was then taken prisoner by Canton, Elliott and party. Shortly before the young man got to the stable the big man came out of the house. I showed up again and took a good look at him, and asked Tisdale who he was. Tisdale said he did not know the man; that he was not wanted by the mob. The big man came out to where there was a big cottonwood tree and took an ax in one hand and began cutting the bark high up on the tree. Shortly after the arrest of the young man the big man quit cutting the bark on the big tree and walked over near a smaller tree. He had been there for perhaps 10 minutes, when there was a shot fired from an aperture in the stable that was used to throw out the manure. Almost at the same time that the first shot was fired from the stable the men stationed at the north end of the barn commenced firing, and those men stationed in different localities fired about the same time. The big man staggered and fell. The mob kept up a continual fire, and the big man commenced crawling on his hand and knees towards the door of the K. C. house. After the mob had fired perhaps 100 shots there was a man appeared in the door of the house, in plain view, and began shooting toward the stable. He fired a number of shots and went out of sight in the house. He disappeared only for a moment and then came out in full view and began shooting again. During this time the mob kept up a constant fire and the big man that was shot near the house kept crawling toward the door. By the time the big man got near the door of the house the small man had shot 10 or 20 shots. The small man then put down his gun and pulled the big man in the house. The mob kept shooting at the house for the balance of the day, and there was a good many shots fired from the house. The mob claimed that the first man shot was Nate Champion. The mob kept the house surrounded and sent to a ranch to get a wagon load of hay to run against the K. C. house to burn it down, but the men came back that had been sent after the wagon and reported that the wagon was away from home. About 3 o'clock a man and a boy came along the road. The man was horseback and the boy was driving the team. The mob told them to throw up their hands and immediately began firing at them. They whipped up their horses, and after going a mile or so they took a horse out of the harness, the boy mounted the horse, and they made their escape, closely followed by some of the mob, who fired a good many shots at them. The mob captured the wagon and horse left behind by the boy and man. They brought the wagon down to the stable and loaded it with brush, hay and wood and pitch pine. Major Wolcott, A. B. Clark, John Tisdale, Tom Smith and James Dudley then run the wagon against the K. C. house and set fire to the hay and shavings on the wagon. The house soon caught fire. There had not been a shot fired from the house for over an hour before the wagon was run against the house. The mob thought that both men in the house might be dead.

In about half an hour after they had run the wagon against the house and set fire to it, a man ran out of the south end of the house and continued running south. The mob at the stable and vicinity kept up a continual fire on the man that came out and was running south. After the man had run about 200 yards and was nearly opposite a part of the mob who were concealed in a gulch south of the house, the mob at the stable and vicinity quit firing, and the part of the mob who were concealed in the gulch south of the house raised up and began firing and killed the man who came out of the house at the K. C. ranch. The man that was killed in the gulch south of the K. C. house the leaders identified as Nate Champion. They said they were mistaken about the first man that was shot in the morning. They said that when they captured the teamsters, Jones and Walker, that Walker told them that there were only two men at the house, Ray and Champion. The mob said the first man shot in the morning must have been Nick Ray. Tom Smith, of the mob, went through Champion's pockets and found a memorandum book, with sketches of the fight at different times during the day. One of the mob took Champion's six-shooter and belt. After Champion's pockets had been rifled, Sam T. Clover, at the request of some of the mob, Tom Smith, Joe Elliott and others, wrote upon a piece of paper, "Beware,

Cattle Thieves!" and buttoned the piece of paper upon Champion's vest. Tom Smith, Elliott and others of the mob said they wanted that piece of paper left on Champion's body so that when his friends found him that they would know what he was killed for, and so that his friends would know what to expect if they stayed any longer in the country.

After the mob had killed Champion and Ray at the K. C. ranch we took supper at the wagons, about half a mile above the K. C. house, on the river. After supper we started for Buffalo. About six or seven miles from the K. C. ranch we changed horses and kept on the road to Buffalo until near a place known as Carr's ranch, where we saw a bright fire burning about half a mile ahead. Some one in the direction of the fire let a gun go off. We then left the road and turned to the left and cut a wire fence and went through a large field, and came into the road again and followed the road to the 28 ranch, where we got some coffee and bread and took two hours' rest in the loft of the stable. We then started for Buffalo on the morning of the 10th of April, and came a short distance toward Buffalo from the T. A. ranch, when Ford, who had gone to the T. A. ranch to get a change of saddle horse for one of the mob by the name of Dudley, came riding up to where the mob had halted, and reported that Dudley's horse had bucked with him and thrown him, and that his Winchester fell out of the scabbard and was discharged about the time that Dudley fell from his horse, and shot Dudley, breaking his leg. The leaders claimed that arrangements had been made with parties in Buffalo to meet them a short distance from Buffalo and inform them as to the state of affairs in Buffalo. While we were talking about what to do with Dudley a man rode up to us. He came from the direction of Buffalo.

This man informed the leaders that there were over 200 settlers in Buffalo up in arms against the mob, and that the settlers were deputized as a sheriff's posse for the purpose of arresting the mob. This horseman informed us that the sheriff was in the Powder river country with a posse looking for the mob. This horseman said that the parties that had charge of the arrangements for assassinating the sheriff at Buffalo had intended to kill the sheriff on the night of the 9th of April, in order to keep the sheriff from organizing sheriff posses before the mob could get to Buffalo. But the horseman said that a man from Powder river had rode into Buffalo on the afternoon of the 9th of April and reported the fight at K. C. ranch, and the man said that the sheriff had organized a posse and started to Powder river before the parties who had intended to kill him had an opportunity to do so. The mob turned back and went to the T. A. ranch and fortified. The leaders claimed the reason they were fortifying at the T. A. ranch was on account of their plans miscarrying in regard to the killing of the sheriff on the night of the 9th of April. The mob intended to kill the sheriff and his deputies, if they first made a raid on Buffalo. But if the mob should get in a fight on the road to Buffalo, so that there was a chance for the people in Buffalo to hear about the mob being in the country before they had time to get to Buffalo, they claimed to have made arrangements with certain parties in Buffalo to assassinate the sheriff and his deputies in order to prevent them from swearing in a large posse of men for the purpose of arresting the mob. About 12 o'clock a party of 15 or 20 men were seen by the mob a short distance from the T. A. ranch going on the road towards Buffalo. The leaders of the mob said the party were the sheriff and posse and gave orders for every man of us to conceal himself and to keep out of sight until the sheriff and posse came up so close that we could see the white of their eyes from the stable, and then the leaders of the mob said for us to open fire on the sheriff and posse, and to kill every one of them. The leaders of the mob claimed that the sheriff and posse would come to the ranch to demand the surrender of the mob, but the sheriff's party kept the road toward Buffalo and did not come to the ranch that day, April 10th, 1892. The leaders claimed that we were safer fortified at the T. A. ranch than anywhere. They said the sheriff at Buffalo would deputize several hundred settlers for the purpose of arresting the mob who would have taken no part in the fight. If the sheriff and deputies had been killed on the night of the 9th of April, according to the arrangements made by the mob with certain parties in Buffalo, the leaders of the mob claimed that it would be impossible for the sheriff's posse to capture us at T. A. ranch inside of a week, and that before that time Governor Barber and Senators Carey and Warren would manipulate the troops at McKinney in such a manner that the troops would come to the rescue of the mob before the sheriff's party could do us any injury. The leaders of the mob were very bitter towards the soldiers at McKinney, and especially the commanding officer. The leaders of the mob said they knew the teamsters and wagons would be captured by the rustlers, and that they had fixed up a good scheme on the old beef-eating vagabond who was in command of the troops at McKinney. They claimed they had told the teamsters to tell everybody that they had orders from the leader to drive the wagons to the post at McKinney and turn them over to the commanding officer at the post according to arrangements that the leaders had made with the commanding officer to take charge of the wagons a week before. About 12 o'clock two men came from Buffalo and joined the mob; one of the men was Phil Du Friend and the other, I understand, was George Sutherland. The men brought considerable news from Buffalo to the mob. The mob claimed the cause of their being obliged to fortify at the T. A. ranch was on account of the sheriff and deputies not having been killed, according to arrangements. They claimed that if the sheriff and deputies had been killed that there would not have been any officers to swear in posse of men as deputy sheriffs for the purpose of arresting the mob, and that the settlers would not have taken the responsibility upon themselves of turning out and fighting the mob. On the other hand, the leaders claimed that if the sheriff and deputies had been killed, according to arrangements made by the leaders of the mob, that their friends would have joined them when we came to Buffalo, and that the expedition would have been a success instead of a possible failure. These matters were talked over by the leaders, Du Friend and the other man from Buffalo.

The leaders explained to Du Friend and the other man that we would be obliged to fortify and remain at the T. A. ranch until Governor Barber, Senators Carey and Warren sent the troops at McKinney to our rescue. The leaders claimed that we could stand the sheriff's posse off for a week if necessary without losing any men, if the friends of the mob in Buffalo would closely watch the soldiers at McKinney and prevent the soldiers at McKinney from stealing out a Gatling gun and turning it over to the sheriff's posse, some of whom the leaders said were ex-soldiers and knew how to work a cannon. The leaders told Du Friend and the other man that the morning of the 11th of April they would send a man from T. A. ranch to Cheyenne to confer with Governor Barber and the officers of the stock growers' association in regard to the predicament the mob was in, and for the purpose of making arrangements with the officers of the stock growers' association to have at least 150 men in readiness to reinforce the mob whenever the officers of the stock growers' association thought it would be expedient. The leaders explained to considerable length to Du Friend and the other man that there was yet a show for the mob to make a success of their raid, if their friends in Buffalo would go to the front as they agreed to. The leaders told Du Friend and the other man that there was a show for the troops from McKinney to come out to the T. A. ranch in the night to stop the fight. The leaders explained to Du Friend and the other man that if some of the friends of the mob could be concealed in a gulch by themselves near the lines of the rustlers and open fire upon the troops from McKinney; that the success of the raid made by the mob depended upon that one circumstance. The leaders said that their friends in Buffalo would have plenty of time to make their own arrangements in regard to selecting their ground, so there would be no trouble for them to get out of the way after they had fired on the soldiers, and the fight had begun between the soldiers and the rustlers. The leaders said that if the friends of the mob could bring on a fight between the soldiers and the sheriff's posse in the night that the mob would have their horses saddled for the occasion, and that as soon as the fight began between the soldiers and sheriff's posse that the mob would mount their horses and make their escape towards Cheyenne, where they would be joined by reinforcements, and would come back and kill every man that had packed a gun against them at the T. A. ranch.

The man that came from Buffalo with Du Friend said he would go back to Buffalo and see what arrangements he could make to bring on a fight between the troops and the sheriff's posse. He left in the afternoon for Buffalo. I asked Du Friend when he first heard the mob was coming to Johnson county. He said the first he knew for a certainty that they would raid the county was last January when he was in Cheyenne. I asked him if he had come from Buffalo to join and stay with them; he said he had. Du Friend said that if the rustlers got a hold of me all they would do would be to shoot me, but he said that if he fell in the rustlers' hands they would burn him. On the afternoon of the 10th of April the mob built their fortifications in order to stand off the sheriff's posse until Governor Barber, Senators Carey and Warren could send the troops at McKinney to the rescue of the mob. The leaders claimed that if they attempted to retreat when their horses were so near played out that they would be surrounded by the sheriff's posse and would have to surrender to the civil authorities—something the mob said they did not propose to do under any circumstances.

On the night of the 10th of April one of the mob came to the T. A. ranch about 10 o'clock in the evening; he said that he was riding in the head teamster's wagon and had his horse saddled and tied behind the wagon; said that sheriff's posse passed the wagons on their road to K. C. ranch; said sheriff's posse asked the head teamster a few questions and then went on. He reported that after sheriff's posse left the wagons he got on his horse and came to join us; he said the country was full of rustlers. About 3 o'clock in the morning of the 11th of April I went from the fort down to the house to get some grub for the men at the fort; at the house I saw a man with his leggins and spurs on; I supposed that he was the man that was going to Cheyenne. I asked Fay Parker who he was, and Wolcott spoke up and said the man's name was Johnnie Jones; that he was a distant relation of a great grand-aunt of his, and that I would better take a good look at him so I would know him the next time I saw him. After I had finished my breakfast at the house I took some grub and coffee up to the men at the fort. About daylight a number of horsemen appeared in sight of the fortifications coming from the direction of Buffalo. The firing then commenced and was kept up most of the time until the surrender of the mob to the troops at Fort McKinney.

During the fight at the T. A. ranch the mob seemed to feel perfectly secure from danger; they claimed that they were so strongly fortified that the sheriff's posse would not charge the works, and that it would be impossible for the sheriff's posse to get their rifle pits close enough to harass the mob before Governor Barber, Senators Carey and Warren would send the troops at McKinney to the rescue of the mob. Then they claimed that if the rustlers and troops did not get into a fight that it would be necessary to surrender to the military authorities and be taken to Fort Russell at Cheyenne, where, the leaders claimed, they would be turned loose in a short time, and they would come back to Johnson county stronger than ever, and would kill every man that packed a gun against them at the T. A. ranch. The leaders seemed to think the possible failure of the raid was due to the fact that the sheriff and deputies were not killed on the night of the 9th of April.

During the fight at the T. A. ranch the mob talked a great deal about the way the men who were in the employ of the stock growers' association last summer and fall had terrorized the settlers; they claimed that last summer and fall there was only four men in the employ of the stock association for the purpose of killing off the rustlers; they claimed these four men were Frank Canton, Tom Smith, Joe Elliott and Fred Coates. Elliott and Canton had a good deal to say about how they would be back after the fight at the T. A. ranch. They said they would terrorize the settlers of Johnson county when they got back again so that those settlers who had an opportunity to leave would get out of the country the best way they could. The troops from McKinney did not arrive quite as soon as the leaders expected; they thought that the commander of the troops was standing in with the sheriff's posse, and had taken the wrong road to the T. A. ranch. When the troops came in sight soon after sunrise the mob appeared in fine spirits, and said that their friends—Governor Barber, Senators Warren and Carey—had sent the troops to their rescue, and that it would be but a short time when they would come back stronger than ever, and would kill off every man that packed a gun against the mob at the T. A. ranch.

GEORGE DUNNING.

STATE OF WYOMING, County of Johnson, ss.:

Personally appeared before me, T. P. Hill, clerk of the District court in and for Johnson county, state of Wyoming, George Dunning, who is personally known to me as the person who signed the foregoing statement, and deposes upon oath, duly adminstered to him, that the foregoing statement by him signed and comprising 44 pages, numbered in red ink from 1 to 44 inclusive, was written by him, is made without solicitation, fear or threats from any party or parties whatsoever, and that all the matters and things contained therein are true to his own knowledge and belief.

GEORGE DUNNING.

Subscribed in my presence and sworn to before me this 6th day of October, 1892.

T. P. HILL,
Clerk District Court.

By GUSTAVE E. A. MOELLER,
Deputy Clerk.